Why Spanking Doesn't Work

Stopping This Bad Habit and Getting the Upper Hand on Effective Discipline

Why Spanking Doesn't Work

Stopping This Bad Habit
and Getting the Upper Hand
on Effective Discipline

by

Michael J. Marshall, Ph.D.

BONNEVILLE BOOKS™

Springville, Utah

ISBN: 1-55517-603-8
v.1

Published by Bonneville Books
Imprint of Cedar Fort Inc.
www.cedarfort.com

Distributed by:

Typeset by Kristin Nelson
Cover design by Adam Ford
Cover design © 2002 by Lyle Mortimer

Printed in the United States of America
10 9 8 7 6 5 4 3 2 1

Printed on acid-free paper

Library of Congress Cataloging-in-Publication Data

Marshall, Michael J., 1949-
  Why spanking doesn't work : stopping this bad habit and getting the upper hand on effective discipline / by Michael J. Marshall.
    p. cm.
  ISBN 1-55517-603-8 (pbk. : alk. paper)
  1. Corporal punishment. 2. Discipline of children. I. Title.
  HQ770.4 .M368 2002
  649'.64--dc21
                        2002006773

Acknowledgments

First and foremost I thank my wife, Mary Kay, for her moral support and logistical help. Without her unwavering and constant support, I would not have been able to complete this manuscript. I am also grateful to West Liberty State College for providing me sabbatical time to work on this project. Eleanor Coen has been a tremendous help by providing secretarial services. David Linden generously provided the use of his rats for the photo illustration. Jordan Riak provided much useful information on the website nospank.net as well as helpful comments about the manuscript. I especially thank him for his excellent ideas and collaboration on writing Chapter 6. Finally, I would like to thank the Cedar Fort, Inc. reviewers for their careful editing and their talented graphics personnel for the cover design.

Dedication

I dedicate this book to the five people who brought me more joy than I ever expected to reap from life, my loving wife, Mary Kay, my four children, Jared, Lara, Hannah, and Sheridan, and all the other children of the world whom, I pray, will receive the life-long gift of being disciplined in a healthy and productive manner.

Table of Contents

Foreword

There is a deadly silence surrounding routine assault and battery of children commonly referred to as "spanking." Dr. Michael J. Marshall's *Why Spanking Doesn't Work: Stopping This Bad Habit and Getting the Upper Hand on Effective Discipline* shatters that silence. This book satisfies two essential requirements: 1) It meets the most rigorous standards for scholarship and 2) it is entirely accessible to the lay reader. Dr. Marshall's new book adroitly exposes the myths and falsehoods that far too many upstanding citizens endorse in order to camouflage their mistreatment of children. He shows the frightening consequences individually and collectively. *Why Spanking Doesn't Work...* is particularly welcome at a time when much of the world is embracing, rather than rejecting, violent solutions. I enthusiastically recommend it to health care professionals, educators, the makers of education policy, and especially parents.

Jordan Riak, Executive Director,
Parents and Teachers Against Violence in Education
(PTAVE)

Chapter 1

What's Wrong with Spanking?

Guess what the most violent institution in America is today. The federal prison system? No. Professional sports? No. The schools? Wrong again. It's the family. Yes, that's right, the family! Your chances of getting assaulted and injured by someone else in your lifetime are greater within your family *by far* than in any other group of people you are likely to be around, unless you are a gang member or soldier in battle. This is a pretty sad commentary about an institution that Americans hold sacrosanct. Why then is the family so violent? One of the main reasons is our belief as a society that physical punishment should be used as a primary means of controlling behavior. It starts with the belief that spanking is good for our children. This is a very curious belief. I wonder who said parents must hurt their kids when disciplining them? The word *discipline* is derived from the Latin root word *disciplina*, which means teaching or learning. The only thing swatting a kid teaches him is that big people control little people with violence. Do we really want to teach our kids that it is good to inflict pain upon others; that if you love someone you may hurt them?

It would make more sense for discipline to be used as a way to *help* children rather than hurt them. When hitting is used as a form of discipline, kids take that message to the bank: striking someone is the preferred method of getting him to do what you want. Is it any wonder that when children grow up and try to cope with the intricacies of close human relationships, that they resort back to one of their earliest, most

1

powerful and profound lessons from childhood, that *might makes right?* At least 16 million Americans are affected by family violence annually. "If violence were a communicable disease, like swine flu, the government would consider it an epidemic," said Richard Gelles, a University of Rhode Island sociologist (UPI, 1986).

The Problem with Spanking

The use of spanking is a very insidious form of discipline because it seems to work in the short term, but in actuality (and this is a point missed by most who use it) it has the opposite effect in the long term. My primary goal in writing this book is to first convince you that spanking is the last thing you want to do to your child and then suggest enough of the more positive approaches through which you will be able to achieve your parenting goals without having to resort to spanking. I use the term *spanking* in a general sense to represent all forms of using corporal punishment on children. This includes: slapping, shoving, shaking, pulling hair, pinching, twisting arms, etc. because essentially they are the same thing to children—getting their bodies hurt with physical punishment—and they will ulti- mately result in the same harmful physical and psychological effects. "Corporal punishment is defined as a painful, inten- tionally-inflicted (typically, by striking a child) physical penalty administered by a person in authority for disciplinary purposes. Corporal punishment can occur anywhere, and whippings, beatings, paddlings, canings, and flogging are specific forms of corporal punishment" (Paintal, 1999). The research clearly shows that spanking does not work the way most parents think it does and that, over time, spanked chil- dren behave much worse than children who are disciplined without being hit (Hyman, 1997).

Spanking is actually a symptom of poor behavior manage- ment. It is something parents default to when they do not have knowledge of more sophisticated and successful behavior-management techniques. The belief that spanking is equivalent to good parenting and good discipline is a myth. I can guarantee that whatever your parenting goals are, they can be achieved much better without spanking. As a matter of fact, spanking will only serve to strongly *interfere* with any possible desirable parenting goals you may have. It will create many more problems than it will ever solve! The vast body of behavioral science research concluding that spanking is harmful to the development of children is one of the best-kept secrets in child psychology (Straus, 1994).

The National PTA supports the effort to abolish corporal punishment and replace it with more positive discipline techniques as reflected in their pamphlet "Corporal Punishment—Myth and Realities."

Myth: Corporal punishment is used only as the last resort.

Reality: Corporal punishment is often the first response even for minor infractions. Teachers and parents need training in nonviolent ways to handle behavior problems.

Myth: Teachers need the right to use corporal punishment to protect themselves.

Reality: Using physical force for self-protection is not considered corporal punishment. School employees have the right to use force to protect themselves or other people from bodily harm, to gain control of a dangerous weapon or to protect property from damage.

Myth: If corporal punishment is banned, the school will be in chaos.

Reality: Again and again, experience has shown that this does not happen. At worst, behavior remains about the same after corporal punishment is abolished. When alternative discipline codes are put in place, disruption is usually significantly reduced.

Myth: The kid must have deserved it.

Reality: Children are paddled for such minor infractions as whis-

pering, giggling or not finishing their milk.

Myth: Corporal punishment is used only on the worst kids.

Reality: The most likely victims of corporal punishment are the most vulnerable, for example: minorities, the smallest boys, children with disabilities.

Myth: A little swat is good for some kids.

Reality: Corporal punishment hurts all kids, victims and witnesses alike. It increases learning problems and decreases student's ability to concentrate and remember. In severe cases, students subjected to corporal punishment exhibit symptoms of Post Traumatic Stress Disorder, similar to the syndrome experienced by Vietnam veterans.

Myth: Corporal punishment prevents unruliness.

Reality: The higher the incidence of corporal punishment in a school, the higher the level of vandalism and delinquency.

Myth: It's okay to use corporal punishment if parents give permission.

Reality: A spanking at school is very destructive to a child's sense of self-worth. It hurts other children, too, by frightening them or sending them the message that violence is a solution to problems. Also, paddling at school sends the message it's okay to hit kids at home.

Myth: Using corporal punishment lets kids know who's in charge.

Reality: The best way to teach self-control is by example. When teachers use corporal punishment, they teach that being "in charge" means physically forcing others into submission.

Myth: I was paddled and it didn't hurt me.

Reality: We all learn by example. Adults most likely to physically punish children are those who were corporally punished as children themselves. Using corporal punishment today continues the cycle into the next generation.

Myth: Corporal punishment is the only way to teach some kids.

Reality: The most difficult children are often the most helpless. They cannot protect themselves. They need help, not hitting. What do we want to teach?

Positive discipline teaches: Right from wrong.

Corporal punishment teaches: Might makes right.

Positive discipline teaches: Self-control.

Corporal punishment teaches: It's okay to strike out in anger.

Positive discipline teaches: Cooperation in resolving conflicts.

Corporal punishment teaches: We control others by force.

Positive discipline teaches: How to assert oneself by stating needs in words.

Corporal punishment teaches: The way to let out dissatisfaction is by physically abusing others.

Positive discipline teaches: Self-esteem, a feeling that "I am part of the solution."

Corporal punishment teaches: Low self-esteem, a feeling that "It's okay for others to hit me."

Positive discipline teaches: Clear expectations and fair consequences.

Corporal punishment teaches: Hurt and humiliation that is often out of proportion to the misbehavior.

Positive discipline teaches: Respect for those in authority and other people.

Corporal punishment teaches: Fear and resentment of authority.

Copyright 1991. Reprinted with permission from
National PTA
330 N. Wabash Ave., Suite 2100
Chicago, IL
60611-3690; www.pta.org.

Parents who still rely primarily upon spanking for discipline are unintentionally harming the development and personalities of their children. A lot of people have told me that kids who are not spanked are not being disciplined. This is a mistaken belief. Just because a child is not spanked does not mean she is not getting any discipline. There exist many different ways of disciplining, punishing, and setting limits for children *without spanking them*. There are published lists available that contain twenty different ways of disciplining a child and not a single one includes spanking (Windell, 1993). Spanking is not discipline. It is punishment, which is destructive. Discipline is constructive. It involves setting limits and teaching the child how to behave within those limits. Punishment does not teach any new behaviors. Its primary purpose in our society is retribution, to make someone pay with pain for an infraction.

Enlightened parents are aware that there are a number of other means of controlling children's behavior that are vastly superior to corporal punishment. They include time-out, nonreinforcement, praise, revocation of privileges, and token economies. These are good alternatives to spanking. When used properly they can be very effective. Why they work and the proper way to administer them is discussed in Chapter 5. If they are administered correctly, then the need for any punishment at all will be minimal. If the behavior modification techniques of positive reinforcement, nonreinforcement, modeling, and behavioral contracts are emphasized in behavior control, instead of the punitive techniques like spanking and other forms of punishment, it will create the best behaving children of all.

Many people have said to me, "I have to spank my child, because it is the only thing that works!" My standard response is "Are you satisfied with the behavior of your kid now?" If the answer is "Yes," then I retort with: "Well, then I guess that means you won't need to spank your child any more!" If the answer is "No," I ask, "How many times have you spanked your kid in the last year?" The number of times is likely to be quite high, sometimes in the hundreds. This cries out for the logical conclusion of: "If spanking works so well, then why do you have to do it so much?"

If spanking is so bad for kids, then why did I turn out okay?

Before describing the detrimental effects of spanking in the following chapters, I would like to qualify what I say: I am not saying that just because a child is spanked he will be a problem child and will go on to be a menace to society in adulthood. The relationship between cause and effect in human behavior is too complex to make simple assertions like that between any two events (Widom, 1989a). The damaging effects of spanking fall on a continuum, that is, the more a child is spanked, the greater will be the damaging effects. Furthermore, these negative effects will be moderated by other conditions present in the household, like the amount of nurturing. Children who are spanked occasionally by an otherwise very supportive and nurturing parent will probably exhibit few of the negative effects of spanking and will have a good chance of growing up to become very successful members of society, *in spite of the fact that they were hit as children*. One should never underestimate the resiliency of the human spirit. It has an amazing ability to rejuvenate itself after adversity.

Do people really know how they would be different if not hit repeatedly by parents while growing up? Would one be more friendly, cheerful, sociable, outgoing, curious, relaxed, forgiving, or charitable? It's impossible to say without controlled studies providing a scientific answer. One thing is clear, though: Those who say, "I was spanked and it didn't adversely affect me," don't know what they are talking about. Social psychologists have shown that people are poor historians in terms of identifying the causes of their own behavior. A typical study in social psychology illustrates this finding: Isen and Levin (1972) conducted a very clever field experiment to isolate one of the variables contributing to altruistic behavior (helping others). They randomly planted a dime on some of the trays in mall phone booths so that twenty shoppers would find it and get to make a free phone call. Twenty others had to use their own money to make their phone calls. As each of the shoppers, who by now had become unwitting subjects in the field experiment, left the phone booth, the experimenters staged an "accident." They had an actor, who was in on the experiment unbeknownst to the subjects, drop a pile of papers in front of each subject, who was walking away from the phone booth, after having completed the phone call. The experimenters wanted to see if finding a dime had any impact on whether or not the mall patron would stop to help the actor pick up the dropped papers, thus providing a measure of altruistic behavior. Sure enough, ninety percent of the travelers who had found the free dime stopped to help the actor pick up her dropped papers, while only five percent of those who had to make their phone calls with their own money stopped to help. The incredible finding here is how much of an impact on shopper's behavior one thin dime, lying passively in the environment, had on the travelers' behavior. It's mere presence determined whether or not each shopper helped a stranger in need. Now for the most amazing finding in this study, and the point I want to make here: When the subjects were asked *why* they stopped to help a stranger pick up the dropped papers, they readily offered all kinds of reasonable explanations for why they assisted a fellow in need, but not one of them *ever mentioned the presence of the dime.* In other words, none of the subjects had any idea why they behaved the way they did. The experimenters went on to conclude that mood was the major determinant of altruism in this situation. The moods were more positive of those who found the money, thus making them feel more charitable toward strangers. The cause of the subjects' behavior was absolutely unrelated to what they themselves believed and reported.

An example will further illustrate the folly of believing that spanking causes people to become better adults. I have a standard response to those who say to me, "Spanking works because I was spanked and I turned out okay." I respond with the question, "Did you ever get bit by a dog when you were a child?" Usually, the answer is "yes." I then inquire, "Do dog bites make kids turn out okay, too?" It is just as ridiculous to give credit for turning out okay to spankings as it is to give the credit for turning out okay to dog bites. Everyone experiences a number of adverse events of one type or another in childhood. If they turn out okay, it's *in spite of* those adverse events, not *because* of them. People who turned out okay after enduring physical pain need to be congratulated for the strength of their character in overcoming adversity, and as survivors of mistreatment, and should not be told it was the cause of their success. If pain and suffering make people into better adults, then we should not only hit them as children, but also advocate exposing children to divorce, poverty, neglect, and car crashes. Then they would really turn out great!

Spanking as a cultural norm

The biggest problem with corporal punishment lies in the general acceptance of a cultural norm that condones spanking, because it has so much potential for abuse. *Spanking is the gateway to child abuse.* Because our society condones spanking as an acceptable form of discipline, it has the effect of dramatically increasing the incidence of child abuse in our culture. Corporal punishment and child abuse are both on the same violence continuum. If a parent or teacher strikes a child, it's called discipline. If a child strikes a parent or teacher, it becomes assault. Irwin Hyman, Director of the National Center for the Study of Corporal Punishment and Alternatives, believes that "when you give people the power to inflict pain on others, it's abused." Many parents don't know when to stop. Hyman says that "many cases of murdered kids started out with parents trying to discipline them." The child abuse rate of parents who approve of physical punishment is four times higher than that of parents who do not approve of physical punishment, a child-abuse rate of 99 per 1,000 vs. 28 per 1,000, respectively (Moore & Straus, 1987). It is too easy for ignorant parents to rationalize child abuse in the name of good discipline (Feshbach, 1980; Graziano, 1989). An example is a recent court case in England. A stepfather caned a twelve-year-old boy so severely that he needed hospital treatment "for gashes on his buttocks, calves, and thighs" (Murray, 1996, p. 10). When the boy's father took the stepfather to court, the jury sided with the stepfather, deciding: "the stepfather had merely been disciplining the boy, not abusing him" (p.10). If it became totally unacceptable to strike a child, the rate of physical child abuse in America would drop dramatically. The cultural norm that condones spanking is an invitation to child abuse. Given the uncritical acceptance of this norm, we would expect severe corporal punishment, defined as *hitting a child with any object*, to be relatively common. Welsh (1978) found this to be the case. He sampled white middle-class PTA members. Forty-two percent of them admitted using a strap on at least one of their children. *Chicago Tribune* columnist, Joan Beck (1987) presents the case for abolishing corporal punishment in the schools.

> CHICAGO—An angry Alabama mother got arrested and charged with assault recently for hitting a teacher on the head with a paddle. The teacher was protected by the law for using the same paddle to hit the 7-year-old son earlier the same day. It's legal—unconscionable, but legal—in [23] states for teachers and school administrators to inflict corporal punishment on children. It's done an estimated 3

million times a year, most often by whacking youngsters with a wooden paddle and most often in elementary school. A surprising number of teachers, school principals and parents consider it an indispensable educational tool, even though some young victims have had to be hospitalized with injuries that would have resulted in jail sentences for child abuse if done by a mother or father.

Laws against child abuse, however, do not apply to schools in most states, although this position is being challenged in several court cases by parents of children injured by those who were supposed to be teaching them academic skills. In 1977, the Supreme Court, which has upheld many students' rights, ruled that corporal punishment is constitutional and acceptable in schools.

The United States is one of only five developed nations to permit schools to inflict corporal punishment. And it is vigorously defended, if no longer to beat the devil out of children in the Puritan tradition, at least to teach them to obey, do their homework and—in a total failure of reason—not to hit others. Even in California and New York, two states which most recently banned corporal punishment in the schools, its supporters fought hard to keep it.

Recently, some church-affiliated day-care centers in North Carolina have battled attempts by the state's Day Care Commission to forbid slapping, spanking and shaking toddlers and preschoolers in their charge. And there was considerable opposition to the resolution the National Education Association passed at its national convention last week declaring that corporal punishment should not be used as a means of school discipline. Inexplicably, corporal punishment is seen as too cruel, too sadistic, too humiliating, too counterproductive for adult criminals. It is banned in prisons and in the armed forces. But a big majority of states views it as all right for adults to use on little children—not only all right, but also educationally sound.

School authorities often allow themselves to be quoted as explaining that corporal punishment is necessary to maintain discipline and order or to get kids to do their homework, or, as one principal said, to get children's attention so they could be taught, as if they were mules in the old story. Surely anyone safe to entrust with the care of children knows better ways to control them and help them learn. Teachers and principals sometimes say, "These kids come from homes where they are hit, and they don't respond to anything else." But that's even more reason to make schools a safe, civilized refuge where children can learn that there are better ways of getting along together and no one inflicts physical hurt on anyone else. Abused children often grow up to abuse their own offspring; schools could do far-reaching good by immersing them in other kinds of behavior.

What corporal punishment does teach children is that violence is acceptable by the strong against the weak and that hitting is an officially-sanctioned way to resolve problems. It creates smoldering resentments that interfere with learning. It pushes some youngsters into a kind of chronic, macho rebellion against school, as evidenced by the fact that the same youngsters often are beaten repeatedly. It can lead to deep-seated psychological problems. Even decades later, many adults still remember fearing school because they dreaded the humiliation and hurt of being paddled, even if they never were.

That corporal punishment has great potential for harm is tacitly acknowledged by laws and regulations that supposedly govern its use in many states. Some states, for example, rule that children cannot be hit in the face. Some limit paddling to administrators, not teachers, and require that an adult witness be present. At least one requires that no other youngsters be present during the punishment, an admission of the humiliation involved. How could it possibly be tolerated at all?

Dozens of expensive studies have been done on education in the last few years. Hundreds of costly recommendations have been made. State legislatures have passed innumerable school reform bills and appropriations. Governors have vied with each other for recognition as leaders in upgrading education. But abolishing corporal punishment isn't on the lists of reforms, even though it corrodes and corrupts the learning process and change would cost nothing.

Surely that's the easiest place to begin to make changes.

Until spanking becomes unacceptable, it's the equivalent of playing with fire. As a society we generally feel it is our duty to find acceptable substitutes for, or at least impose some controls upon, those things that are very dangerous and have a high likelihood of being misused. Examples are: chemical warfare, nuclear proliferation, drugs, toxic waste, and arms sales. We just don't feel comfortable if anybody on the block is allowed to stockpile plutonium, barrels of toxic PCBs, missile launchers, and Uzi assault rifles. Naturally we just can't make ourselves believe that everyone is mature enough and wise enough to responsibly handle these types of dangerous hardware, so we have no qualms about imposing societal restrictions upon their availability.

I believe that accepting the premise that it is just fine for anyone to use corporal punishment on children is the psychological equivalent of arming every parent with weapons of warfare to be used against their kids. Just look at the statistics that show how this form of discipline affects our children. They amply support this argument: At least 2,000 children are killed every year in the United States by parents who claim they were just exercising their parental duty to discipline their children with physical punishment. The National Family Violence Surveys show that parents severely assault at least 1.7 million children each year (Straus & Yodanis, 1995). Zigler and Hall (1989) estimate that sixty percent of child abuse cases began as physical punishment. About 142,000 are seriously injured each year, adding hundreds of millions of dollars to the cost of medical care (Cavaliere, 1995). An additional 5.4 million children are struck with objects (Straus & Yodanis, 1995). And this is just the tissue damage that the belief in physical punishment results in! The psychological damage is incalculable. This is a tragedy upon our children of almost biblical proportions. If it were caused by anything other than parental discipline we would declare it a national emergency and marshal copious resources to attack the problem. I believe that these shocking statistics will never change unless we first change the general societal attitude that says it is okay and proper for parents to physically hurt their children in the name of discipline. Welsh (1979) examined the cycle of violence handed down from parents to children. He noticed that delinquents invariably were harshly disciplined, and he inquired about the type of "discipline" received by their parents when they were children.

> These parents of delinquents have reported having been beaten with such items as: belts, fists, sticks, cat-o'nine-tails, extension cords, wooden spoons, broom handles, two-by-fours, rubber hoses, and "anything my parents could pick up." Clearly, parents learn to discipline from their own parents and not from child-rearing manuals. One of my patients was a fifteen-year-old boy who had broken into four houses, stolen a gun—shooting it randomly into several houses—and tied a boy to a tree with wire, then beat him with a stick. In describing her childhood, his mother reported, "My father was an alcoholic, worked at a rubber company, and made cat-o'-nine-tails out of rubber strips he brought home. He was very abusive, and we were all terrified of him. My husband [only got] beaten with the belt." The mother of a fifteen-year-old boy who had stolen two cars, broke into a house, and claimed to have had fist fights with his father, reported, "My mother knocked my teeth out with a hairbrush. She used to hit me with a belt, a wooden spoon . . . anything she could get her hands on."

I'm sure that if you asked these parents if they were abusing their children, they would indignantly retort with, "Of course not! I'm just disciplining them." Their conception of what constitutes discipline was learned from their parents and is being handed down to their children.

Given the fact that the technology of behavior control has

advanced to very sophisticated and effective levels, for all intents and purposes, anyone who still hits children should be considered a child abuser by ignorant default. If you have trouble buying this notion, then just ask yourself, "If someone hit me, what would my reaction be?" Let's say you drop a cigarette butt in the airport and airport security comes up and slaps you across the face. Or you are pulled over for speeding and the officer cracks you with a baton for not obeying the speed limit. What if you did not get done what your boss asked you to do and he punished you with ten strokes on the behind with a paddle? Would you like it if your spouse spanked you every time you did something wrong? What would your reaction be in each of these cases? File assault charges? File a complaint for police brutality? Sue? Of course! You know it is not right for someone to physically strike you. This protection from physical assault by others is built into our legal system *for everyone but children*. Why do adults insist upon subjecting children to a form of punishment that they would not impose upon themselves? The following Supreme Court majority opinion defies logic:

An examination of the Amendment and the decisions of this Court construing the proscription against cruel and unusual punishment confirms that is was designed to protect those convicted of crimes. We adhere to this long-standing limitation and hold that the Eighth Amendment does not apply to the paddling of children as a means of maintaining discipline . . . (U.S. Supreme Court, 1977).

Can you imagine that? Corporal punishment is considered to be too cruel and unusual for criminals, but the Supreme Court thinks it is just fine for use on innocent children! I suspect that the only reason children are the last group of people in the U.S. to still be subjected to corporal punishment is that they are the politically weakest. Children cannot vote or lobby and are therefore, when their Eighth Amendment rights are violated, not a threat to legislators.

Spanking a child is just as wrong as slapping a wife. Feminists have worked hard to help women understand that no one deserves to be hit and no one should tolerate it. Hitting a spouse is a crime. As early as 1655 The Massachusetts Bay Colony declared by edict that "No man shall strike his wife." Many early states and territories banned hitting wives with punishments ranging from $1,000 fines to five years in prison. Since 1857 U.S. military officers have not been permitted to strike soldiers. By 1870 the U.S. courts stopped recognizing the common law principle that a husband had the right to "physically chastise an errant wife." In 1890 the corporal punishment of prisoners was outlawed. Now, a century later, it's time to do the same for children—afford them the same protection that adults take for granted. Today, physical punishment is considered too severe for prisoners, soldiers, juvenile delinquents, and spouses. But, we still consider it acceptable to subject innocent children to it. No child deserves to be physically assaulted. Spanking or slapping a child is an act of violence. It indicates that the parent is just as out of control as the child.

Recently, a sensational corporal punishment case made the national news. A mother slapped her teenage daughter, who then filed assault charges against her mother. This landmark case galvanized the country into two camps, those who sided with the mother's right to use corporal punishment and those who were outraged at the mother's actions. Isn't this an interesting situation? Parents slap their kids every day, perhaps hundreds or thousands of times on a nation wide basis. Why did this one case capture people's attention and provoke discussion? It's because the adolescent daughter was neither child nor adult, she was caught in the no-man's land between the state of childhood and adulthood. That's the only reason it became an issue. If she was clearly a child, there would have been no problem because virtually no one believes that striking a child is assault. If she was clearly an adult, no one would have questioned the assault charges because adults have legal protection against assault. But clearly, she's the same person, and should be afforded the same legal protection, whether she's two, ten, fifteen, eighteen, or thirty years old. Logically, why should children not have the same right to be protected from blows by others as we adults do? If anything, because they are so much more innocent and fragile than adults, children should be protected even more! If corporal punishment is unacceptable for adults in a civilized society, "it should (not) become any more acceptable just because it is inflicted upon children" (minority dissenting opinion, U.S. Supreme Court, 1977). A recent newspaper article illustrates the persuasiveness of this breach of logic (Mattice, 1995).

Poll: Spanking Okay, But Don't Hit Wife

CHARLESTON, WV (AP)—West Virginians overwhelmingly believe in spanking their children. But, on the more serious issue of domestic violence, most say police should get involved, even if a person is not actually struck, according a West Virginia Poll.

And 90 percent of West Virginians say it is never all right to strike a spouse, the poll found. While some say spanking is wrong, 85 percent of West Virginians approve of parents spanking their children and only 12 percent disapprove, according to the poll.

But, the poll also found: Senior citizens are more likely to favor it than young adults. High school dropouts are more likely to favor it than college graduates. Poorer people are more likely to favor it than richer people.

Southern West Virginians, 90 percent, and north central West Virginians, 88 percent, are more likely to approve of spanking children than people in the Northern Panhandle, where only 71 percent approve, according to the poll.

Also, men, 89 percent, are more likely to approve of spanking than women, 82 percent, the poll found.

Reprinted with permission of The Associated Press.

Should the "experts" tell you how to raise your kids?

I would not be presumptuous enough to say that the "experts" know how to do a better job of parenting than you do, because they don't. There are no authorities. There is only information. It is up to parents to obtain information and make use of it as they see fit. Parenting is still an art that is too complex for behavioral scientists to fully understand. Scientists may completely understand it in one hundred years and be able to say, "This is the best way to parent," but right now they can't.

Generally, most parents do a satisfactory job of parenting. I am sure most parents have acquired a lot of knowledge about good parenting and what they don't know will more than be compensated for by all the caring and loving they show toward their children. Parents have particular ideas about what they want to accomplish with their children and how to go about it. I do not want to interfere with those preferences because they are what is cherished and right for each person's unique parenting style. Bruno Bettelheim (1987), the late eminent child psychologist, urged parents to throw away their child psychology books. He believes parents have the edge over professionals in solving their children's behavior problems because they are more intimately familiar with what goes on between themselves and their child. He says the solutions parents themselves devise are superior to those of authorities because they are more apt to be "in character" for the family and tailored to their unique situation.

Dr. Bettelheim is not totally disparaging of the experts, though. He believes their strength lies more in uncovering *general* principles of development that parents can then learn about and adapt to their specific needs. I agree with him on this point. If this is true, then what can I offer you in this book? My intention is not to teach parents how to parent, but to communicate to parents a general principle concerning discipline and behavior that is one of the most powerful in all of *psychology—that the results are far superior when behavior is managed by using a positive approach, such as rewarding a desirable behavior, than when a negative approach, such as punishment, is used.* If you already understand and use this principle then there is probably not much the experts could tell you about how to parent. If you are not clear about how or why this principle works, then keep reading. The better you understand it, the better a parent you are likely to be. I have read through the voluminous literature that behavioral scientists have published reporting the outcome of their experiments on corporal punishment. I have attempted to summarize these findings in a readable and accessible format for anyone interested in this issue.

The prevalence of spanking

Unfortunately, the most common type of parental discipline used in America today is spanking. Surveys report that eighty to ninety percent of parents spank their children (Bryan & Freed, 1982; Daley, 1988; Graziano & Namaste, 1990; Sears, Maccoby, & Levin, 1957; Straus, 1983; Wauchope & Straus, 1990). Most people do not see anything wrong with this. As a matter of fact, the opposite is true. Parents who do not spank their children are seen as suspect—maybe they're too permissive; they're spoiling their kids; their kids will be unmanageable; or the kids will grow up to be delinquents. After all, the Bible tells us that we must spank our kids or we are not following the word of God: "Spare the rod and spoil the child."

Isn't that how the saying goes? Many parents feel it is their Christian duty to spank their kids. I believe these are cultural myths and I will refute them at length in later chapters.

This is how the state of our cultural beliefs stands on the issue of spanking and disciplining our children today: Americans widely believe that spanking is equivalent to good parenting. This is the message that is transmitted to those who grow up in our culture and do not pursue any further knowledge about the topic. Since most people do not study anything formally about parenting in school, this is where their knowledge of discipline ends. They are not aware of any of the thousands of studies that have been conducted by social and behavioral scientists—studies that contain a lot of important information that parents can use to be more effective disciplinarians and studies that provide answers to questions like: *Is spanking the best type of discipline to use on my child? How do I handle a tantruming two-year-old? What should I say to my child when I discipline? What infractions warrant punishment? Can spanking be harmful to my child? And, are there effective alternatives to spanking?* How do researchers know which method of discipline is most effective? The following section explains how psychologists, sociologists, and other social scientists come up with answers to these questions.

How social scientists research punishment

It would not be ethical for a psychologist to conduct an experiment of the effects of spanking on children directly, because in order to do so, the psychologist would first have to randomly divide children into two groups, one of which would be harmed. One group would not get any spankings and the psychologist would have to regularly spank (or see to it that the parents would) the kids in the other group. The Institutional Ethics Review Board would not allow that type of experiment to be conducted because it would require that children be hit by adults as part of the study. Under these experimental conditions, hitting children is considered unethical along the lines of the Nazi human medical studies of World War II.

If a psychologist wanted to conduct an experiment to study the effects of spanking on behavior, she would have to use an animal model like a rat. However, there is still a problem with studying spanking when using animal models. It would appear kind of ridiculous for a psychologist to be picking up rats and spanking them everyday. It would also be scientifically imprecise and sloppy. Therefore, the best way to study spanking experimentally with animals is to use a more precise measure of physical punishment, like shock. Conceptually it is identical to spanking because they are just two different ways of inflicting physical pain. If the punished rats behave differently than the unpunished rats, we can attribute the difference in behavior to the effects of punishment, using this research technique, which is called the *experimental research method*. This is one way to find out how punishment affects behavior because it is such a powerful research technique. It allows the researcher to determine *cause and effect*, that is, what it is that causes a particular behavior to occur. For instance, are children who are spanked more or less aggressive than those who are not spanked? We could use the experimental technique on an animal model to try to provide answers.

However, one has to first be convinced that the study of rat behavior can provide answers about human behavior. Do the studies of rat behavior generalize to human behavior? That is, will humans behave the same as rats do when they are punished? Probably not exactly, because humans are so complex. Their possible ways of responding outnumber what rats are capable of doing. A major issue associated with the field of comparative psychology, the study of animal behavior as a means of better understanding human behavior, is that some people do not believe that understanding animal behavior can tell us anything about human behavior. However, there is quite a bit of evidence that studying animal behavior can tell us a lot about human behavior, sometimes more than studying humans alone! Animal models of behavior provide several benefits over studying humans. The first benefit was already mentioned above. We can conduct studies on animals that would be considered unethical with humans, PETA's concerns (People for the Ethical Treatment of Animals) aside. Also, animal results are simpler to interpret and understand.

People are so complex that they contaminate experiments in unexpected ways: For instance, there are subject effects, where participants in experiments unconsciously try to please the experimenter by guessing the hypothesis and conforming to it in the study. People are also devious. They give socially desirable responses rather than honest ones to such questions as "What is your income," "Have you ever stolen from your employer," "Have you ever cheated on your income taxes," "Do you always tell the truth," and "How often do you attend church?"

Animals do not lie. What you see is what you get. There are fewer complexities and this fact has served psychologists well. An example comes from learning theory. Psychologists spent half a century trying to understand such basic human functions as learning with a research method called *introspection*, in which they asked humans in experiments to verbally report how they learned things. That method of study ended in a dismal failure because people, as they came to realize, have practically no idea why they behave the way they do and are masters at distorting their motives (Myers, 2002).

Introspection was discarded and replaced with *behaviorism*. Behaviorists believed that what happened in the mind was worthless, that only behavior need be observed in order to completely understand behavior. This method of study proved spectacularly successful for such pioneering learning researchers as Ivan Pavlov, Edmund Thorndike, and B. F. Skinner. Through observing the reactions of dogs, cats, pigeons, and rats to controlled learning situations such as mazes, they were able to uncover the laws of learning. What's so amazing about their findings is what psychologists refer to as *general process learning theory.* The laws of learning work identically in all organisms from the simplest, such as a worm, to the most complex—humans. No matter which of the millions of species of animals that exist on earth are tested, the principles of learning always work in an identical fashion on all of them! A planarian worm can be trained to react in a classically-conditioned fashion to a light that signals a shock is coming in the same way one can classically condition a rat, horse, person, or any other organism. This is the type of evidence that makes psychologists comfortable with generalizing the results of animal studies to humans.

The other main research technique psychologists use to study spanking and other types of physical punishment is called the *correlational study.* In this method they just find parents who do and do not use physical punishment and compare the behaviors of their children. Using this method is a little more tricky than the experimental method because it is more difficult to determine cause and effect, but it can still provide useful data, particularly as a predictor of behavior. Most of the studies reported in the following chapters utilize one or the other of these two main behavioral research methods.

Let us begin now, in the next three chapters, to explore the research that provides an answer to one of the most important questions posed above, "Can spanking be harmful to my child?" The answer is a very emphatic "yes." There exists copious evidence that spanking damages children (Gershoff, 2002). Amazingly, it does so in thirteen different ways! Psychologists call these the *unintended adverse side effects of punishment*. They are summarized below.

The 13 Ways Spanking Harms Children:

1. **Creates aggression**. Children who are spanked engage in more hitting and fighting than those who are not physically punished by their parents.

2. **Lowers self-esteem**. Spanking sends a message to kids that says, "You are a bad person who deserves pain and you are not valuable enough to protect from being hurt," which is incorporated into their self-concept.

3. **Creates negative affect (bad feelings).** Physical punishment results in feelings of fear, anxiety, humiliation, and depression. In extreme cases it can lead to such disorders as sociopathy and posttraumatic stress disorder. Children become very confused emotionally when the person they expect to love and care for them periodically flip-flops and deliberately hurts them.

4. **Alienates the child from the parents**. People naturally try to avoid a source of physical punishment, resent the perpetrator, and generally do not like or feel good about the person who is responsible for it. Likewise, children may come to associate the punisher with the punishment and end up being fearful of and try to avoid the parent.

5. **Creates suppression effects**. Kids who receive a lot of physical punishment are less spontaneous, more reserved, and afraid to try new things out of fear that it will result in more punishment.

6. **Contributes to antisocial behavior**. Spanking teaches children that the motive for desired behaviors is concern

for the consequences to one's self, that is, to avoid pain, rather than be concerned for the effects of one's behavior on others.

7. **Creates masochistic tendencies**. Through the conditioning process, children who are hurt by those who love them will come to associate pain with love.

8. **Hinders learning and achievement**. Children who have had a lot of physical punishment do poorly in school, perform more poorly on tests of development, graduate from college at a lower rate, and earn less money.

9. **Models undesirable behaviors**. Children of parents who use hitting as their primary means of controlling behavior learn that "might makes right" and are less likely to acquire nonviolent conflict resolution skills.

10. **The undesirable behavior is not eliminated**. The unwanted behavior is only temporarily suppressed in the presence of the punisher. Through discrimination learning a child quickly learns that she can get away with engaging in the wrong behavior whenever the punisher is not present to act as an enforcer.

11. **Makes children more likely to engage in the forbidden behaviors**. Children brought up with physical punishment have higher levels of *reactance*, which is the desire to engage in those behaviors which are prohibited, than those who are disciplined nonphysically.

12. **Raises the punishment threshold**. Children can eventually adapt to a given level of punishment and it will lose its intended effect. This forces the punisher to constantly increase the intensity of punishment in order for it to have any effect. The increased level of physical punishment then makes them become jaded to being struck by others and more likely to accept abusive relationships as normal.

13. **Causes physical injuries**. Pediatricians are alarmed at the number of injuries they see, like radial arm fractures and Shaken Child Syndrome, which result from the actions of parents who physically strike or shake their children.

Advice from *Dear Abby* (1993) reflects an awareness of these harmful side effects.

DEAR ABBY: As a child advocate for a battered women's and children's shelter, I would like to commend you for sticking to your response to the man who slapped his fourteen-year-old son across the face for calling him a filthy name. I have read the many letters you received from people who supported and justified the slap. Thanks for not backing down! I would also like to add something that is posted in our shelter concerning the subject:

"When parents hit a child, they are teaching the following:

1. Might makes right.

2. People who love you hurt you, therefore love hurts.

3. Power and control get you what you want in life.

4. Violence is an appropriate problem-solving technique.

5. Reser.tment, hatred, denial and confusion.

Remember this: If it is inappropriate for a batterer to hit, push and shove a partner, then it is inappropriate for a parent to do the same thing to a child."

On behalf of children, thanks!

Jennifer Richardson,

Tri-state Coalition Against Family Violence

Keokik, Iowa

DEAR JENNIFER: Thank you for a valuable contribution. I am publishing it in the hope that those who need the reminder will clip it.

As seen in Dear Abby *by Abigail Van Buren a.k.a. Jeanne Phillips and founded by her mother Pauline Phillips. ©Universal Press Syndicate. Reprinted with permission. All rights reserved.*

Are you surprised by this list? I was, when I first read about the unintended impact of punishment on behavior. I have found that very few people have any idea of the full impact of their actions when they spank their children. I want parents to be aware of these findings because I want them to be fully aware of what they are doing to their kids. I want them to make informed choices. If they choose to discipline with corporal punishment, they might as well know that they are playing Russian roulette. Since human behavior is probabilistic in nature, some spanked kids may not exhibit any of these undesirable behaviors, but then again, wouldn't it be foolish to take the risk?

Chapter 2

Spanking and Aggression in Your Child

Consider the implications of the following conversation:

Parent: I'm at my wits end about the way Junior acts at school. They are constantly calling me about his bad behavior. His teacher says he terrorizes the classroom with his constant hitting and fighting.

Sympathetic Listener: Maybe he needs more discipline.

Parent: He's the most disciplined child in the world. I spank him all the time!

Why does Junior continue to act aggressively even though he is regularly punished? The research of psychologists, sociologists, and other social scientists suggests that he has been taught to be aggressive by his parents when they spank him and he is simply imitating their behavior by resorting to physical violence when confronted with a problem. This constitutes the first behavioral problem the use of physical punishment creates. In the next three chapters, the research that finds "spanking is harmful to children in thirteen different ways" will be summarized, in order, starting with the first negative side effect: aggression. I am using the term "aggressive" here in the pejorative sense, that is behavior that is unacceptably violent. I just want to differentiate between this meaning of the word *aggressive* and the other positive sense in which it can be used. Sometimes people use the word to indicate a positive personality trait as in, "We are looking for a very aggressive salesperson to take over our Southeastern sales territory." The thirteen undesirable side effects of spanking will be examined, starting with the most heavily researched, the effects of punishment on aggression.

Undesirable Side Effect of Spanking #1

Spanking creates aggressive behavior in children

The laboratory research of Albert Bandura, an eminent learning psychologist and proponent of the social learning theory of aggression, has shown that children readily learn to imitate the aggressive behavior of adults (Bandura et al., 1961). He reached this conclusion by conducting his famous Bobo doll experiments. In the Bobo experiment he had one group of children watch an adult attack an inflated plastic figure—hitting, kicking and throwing it while shouting, "Sock him in the nose! Hit him down! Kick him!" Another similar group of children, the control group, was not exposed to the violent adult behavior. Next, both groups of kids were brought to another building and put in a room full of attractive toys where they were told they could not play with them. The kids were given a few minutes to reflect on their predicament, being in a room full of neat toys and told they were not allowed to play with them. Shortly, the experimenters moved them to a room next door that contained both aggressive toys, which included the Bobo doll, and nonaggressive toys. In contrast to the children in the control group, who ended up playing calmly with these toys, those who had previously witnessed the adult's aggressive behavior lashed out at the Bobo doll in an amazing manner— they almost exactly reproduced the very acts and words of the aggressive adult models.

This study highlights one of the most powerful research findings on the effects of punishment—that it creates aggressive behavior. In the Bandura experiment the aggressive behavior was learned. Owens and Straus (1975) tested Bandura's theory of observational learning on the creation of violent attitudes. They hypothesized that, "The greater the observation of violence as a child, the greater the approval of violence in adult life" and "The more a child is a victim of violence in childhood, the greater his approval of violence in adult life" (p. 198). They examined data from the National Commission on the Causes and Prevention of Violence survey in which 1,176 adults were randomly sampled from the U.S. population and interviewed. Their hypotheses were supported. They found that those children who were exposed to violence in childhood, such as seeing others slapped, punched, or choked, and those who received violent treatment in childhood such as being spanked, slapped, punched, or choked reported more favorable attitudes toward violence as adults. They were more likely to approve of such violent acts as spanking a noisy child, a husband slapping his wife for flirting, a teacher hitting a disobedient student, and a police officer striking a demonstrator.

Dr. Murray Straus, a sociologist, and his colleagues conducted a longitudinal study in 1998 that addressed the chicken-and-egg issue: Which comes first, aggression or physical punishment? Do parents hit aggressive kids more because they are more likely to get into trouble or do children who are physically punished by their parents become more aggressive as a result of being hit? He conducted interviews with 809 mothers across the country. He assessed the degree of antisocial behavior exhibited in their children by asking the mothers to answer such questions as how much each child "bullies or is cruel or mean to others" and "cheats or tells lies." The amount of spanking received by the children was also recorded. After two years, the children's antisocial behavior was measured again. Straus found that the more the children were spanked, the more antisocial they became. This effect held true even for those children that were spanked as little as once a week and received a lot of love and intellectual stimulation at home.

However, the aggressive response to punishment may also have another component that is even more basic than that. There is evidence that an aggressive response to punishment is innate as well. There appears there is an innate pain-attack reaction. In an early classic experiment done by two psychologists, Ulrich and Azrin (1966), rats were placed in a Skinner Box (cage) with an electrified grid floor. The rats' behavior was observed under two conditions, with and without shock. When no shock was administered, the rats just wandered around the cage as they normally would and did not attempt to hurt each other. However, when the rats were administered shock through the electrified grid floor, they always behaved in the same fashion; they were driven into a violent attack on each other, where they would fight to the point of drawing blood. In the researchers' words:

> When two Sprague-Dawley rats were first placed in the experimental chamber, they moved about slowly, sniffing the walls, the grid, and occasionally each other. At no time did any fighting behavior appear in the absence of shock. Soon after shock was delivered, a drastic change in the rats' behavior took place. They would suddenly face each other in an upright position, and with the head thrust forward and the mouth open they would strike vigorously at each other . . . (Ulrich & Azrin, 1966, p. 503).

The more intense the shock, the more violent was the rats' aggression. The attack response never faded, even after enduring several thousand shocks a day. The rats would attack anything—it didn't matter what. They would just as readily attack different species, stuffed toys, or even a tennis ball! This finding has been replicated many times and with many other types of animals including crayfish, snakes, pigeons, squirrels, raccoons, cats, foxes, dogs, and monkeys (Schwartz, 1989). The cruelty of the animals to each other seemed to match the amount of pain imposed upon them. Even people are not immune from this reaction. Students whose hands were kept in painfully cold water were more willing to punish others by blasting them with an unpleasant noise, compared to students whose hands were dunked in lukewarm water (Berkowitz, 1989). There seems to be a pain-produced attack that is fast and consistent in all species which operates in the same "push-button" fashion as occurred with the rats.

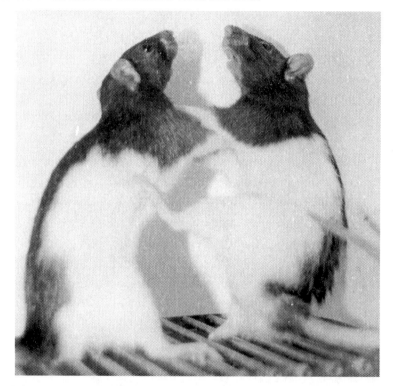

Figure 1. Example of stereotypical fighting posture assumed by rats when shocked (Ulrich & Azrin, 1966). *Photo by Mike Marshall.*

What are the implications of these findings for real life situations? Just remember back to the last time someone struck you. What was your reaction? If it was similar to mine, then you felt an intense rush of anger and a strong desire to strike back. In high school once during P.E., while playing basketball, a player from the opposite team elbowed me aggressively. I instinctually lashed out at him and clobbered him in retaliation. How often does this scene play out in professional sports? One can think of many other analogous human situations. Once, as a teenager, a friend and I were traveling. There was no public transportation for the last twenty miles to our destination, so we had to walk. Unfortunately we were ill-prepared to do so. It was a desolate section of highway, the temperature was over one hundred degrees, we had no water, we were getting sunburned, and our shoes were causing blisters. To top everything off we had to skirt around tarantulas that were periodically crossing the road. At first we just stepped around them and let them cross peacefully. But then, after about three hours of misery, pain, and frustration, my friend, Steve, changed. Upon spotting another tarantula, he ran over the side of the road, grabbed handfuls of gravel and violently blasted the tarantula with the gravel until it was reduced to nothing but scattered remnants. In disbelief I screamed, "Why did you have to do that!" After all, the tarantulas were not harming us. His response was, "I was so miserable it just made me feel better to attack something." I realize this is a bizarre example of this phenomenon but the rat studies explain my traveling companion's behavior very nicely. He was experiencing acute physical pain and reacted violently by striking out at another living organism, just as the rats had done in the Skinner Box.

Brezina (1998) found that the use of corporal punishment increases the probability that children will assault their parents in retaliation, particularly as they grow older. An extreme example of this occurred locally. A teenager shot four arrows into his mother's head with his crossbow while she was sleeping. His defense at his murder trial was that she was physically abusive to him and his anger drove him to retaliate against her.

Another, more mundane, example comes from watching videos on television of police arresting protesters. Invariably when the protester gets rough, or the police do, there is a tit-for-tat escalation in the amount of struggling, hitting and violence exhibited by both parties. The fighting rats research finding also can explain prison riots. Prisons, by nature, are very punitive places. The above animal experiments would predict that the inmates would eventually behave violently under the confined and punitive conditions that cause discomfort. All one has to do is read the newspaper to see that this prediction is supported by actual events. Prison riots are a regular occurrence, many being very sensational and memorable such as Attica in New York, causing 42 deaths in 1971, New Mexico Federal Penitentiary with 33 deaths in 1980, and the more recent prison uprising in Lucasville, Ohio, where 10 deaths occurred in 1993. The Attica prison riot resulted in a twenty-five-year-long lawsuit that was finally settled January 4th, 2000, for eight million dollars awarded to the inmates to compensate for the overzealous punishment at the hands of guards. Former inmate Frank Smith described what happened to him: He said he was beaten and burned by officers. They told him to hold a football under his chin. If it fell, the officers told him, he would be killed. Hundreds of inmates were beaten by correctional officers with clubs while forced to run a gauntlet. Saladin Hadid recalled, "They beat you to your knees, called you degrading things" (AP, 2000). Of course other factors certainly also contributed to the violent outbursts, such as the criminal nature of the inmates, frustration, and various other social-psychological factors. But there is evidence that shows the punitive nature of the prison environment itself is aggravating prisoners' violent tendencies. Serving time in a prison environment makes offenders twice as likely to engage in future criminal activity (Eichmann, 1966).

Journalist Nancy Shulins (1986) searches for an answer to the question, "How do lives go so wrong so soon?"

LOS ANGELES (AP)—On a March afternoon in Miami Beach, a five-year-old boy and a three-year-old neighbor were playing in a high-rise apartment building. While their parents talked in another room, the children wandered out onto the fifth-floor balcony. There, the older child gave his playmate a couple of shoves, the second of which sent the younger boy to his death. When the police arrived, officers said, the smiling 5-year-old readily confessed. He then polished off two slices of pizza, a garlic roll, and a banana . . .

How does a life go so wrong so soon? There are precious clear-cut answers. Experts suspect that the violent behavior of children that erupts into murder is rooted in family relationships gone awry, in frequent rounds of domestic violence, in parental mismanagement of discipline . . .

"Punitive, harsh discipline does not prevent crime," Elliott Currie, a former Yale University criminologist, has written. Currie calls abuse and neglect in childhood "among the most powerful sources of serious criminal activity in American today." High rates of violence in the family, spouses who hit one another and parents who administer harsh punishment to their children all significantly foreshadow aggressive behavior in children, Kazdin said. In about one third of the families being treated at the Pittsburgh Western Psychiatric Institute and Clinic, he said, there is documented child abuse. There is a lot more that we can't find legally. Most of them tend to punish heavily, fail to reward good behavior, scream, and give commands," Kazdin said. Children from violent homes differ from other children in various ways. Despite normal IQs, they often lag behind in school and frequently develop reading problems. They tend to be more easily discouraged than their peers, and are less apt to be artistic or athletic. They also are hard-pressed to make friends. Their violent home life instills in them what sociologists call a "mean world" philosophy. They are quicker than other children to perceive hostility on the part of others and to respond in kind. This makes a fertile breeding ground for more violence.

Reprinted with permission of The Associated Press.

Perhaps the most persuasive evidence that using physical punishment to discipline children leads to aggression comes from the study of bullies (Olweus, 1978, 1979, 1980; Floyd & Levin, 1987). These researchers consistently find that school bullies are almost always victims of harsh physical punishment at home. Olweus speculates that this triggers a process that leads to aggressing against others. Ideally, children should develop a sense of strength and independence as they grow up. However, this process is short-circuited in a home where the parents humiliate and batter the child. When this happens, it makes the battered children feel vulnerable and they hate the feeling. When they encounter another child who exhibits vulnerability, it activates their inner feelings of humiliation and shame. Due to the aggressive responses they have learned in their home environments and their identification with the aggressor parent, they react with hostility rather than compassion. This is what triggers their bullying response. They try to mask underlying feelings of inadequacy, and the fear that they are not in control, by overcompensating with the opposite actions. As adults, researchers found, childhood bullies ended up with less desirable jobs and got into trouble with the law more often than nonbullies. They were also more likely to abuse their wives and discipline their own children with severe physical punishment (Huesmann, Eron & Yarmel, 1987). Journalist William Hidlay (1987) reports on the findings of a bully outcome study published in *The Journal of Personality and Social Psychology*.

CHICAGO (AP)—Parents should discourage their children from acting aggressively, says an author of a twenty-two-year study which found that young bullies grow up to be less successful and hold lower paying jobs. "I think there's a very important message for parents: The traditional view that assertiveness and aggression leads to high achievement and success does not hold up under scrutiny, " said Rowell Huesmann, a co-author of the study and psychology professor at the University of Illinois-Chicago.

Huesman and another Illinois-Chicago psychologist, Leonard Eron, found that third-grade bullies had weaker intellectual and professional achievement at age thirty than non-aggressive class-mates with the same intelligence level. "They were less likely to be professionals, say lawyers or doctors or professors," Eron said in a telephone interview. "The aggressive children were more likely to have blue-collar jobs or to be unemployed or to be in jail."

The psychologists reached those conclusions in a follow-up study of about 300 adults who were tested for aggression and intelligence in 1960 as third-graders in Columbia County, NY In the study, the eight-year-old children were given IQ tests and rated for aggression based on whether they fought with classmates, pushed and shoved or irri-tated other students by taking their property. Aggressive behavior was defined as an act that injures or irritates another child. In the follow-up study, when the participants were thirty, the researchers found that those who were aggressive children scored lower on standard achievement tests than classmates of equal intelligence.

"What we found was that aggression in childhood actually inter-fered with the development of intellectual functioning and was predictive of poorer intellectual achievement as an adult," Eron said.

The professors reported their latest findings in the Journal of Personality and Social Psychology. The study also found a correlation between spanking or other corporal punishment in the home and physical aggression in school, Eron said. "What you're doing when you're spanking them is showing them the way you get what you want is by hitting," he said. As an alternative, Eron recommended that parents use non-physical punishments to discipline children.

Reprinted with permission of The Associated Press.

Spanking is by nature a violent act. The children of parents who use physical punishment are twice as likely to hit their siblings as the children of parents who use nonviolent means to discipline their children (Wolak, 1996). Other research has discovered that children raised by abusive, punishing parents are more likely than other children to become abusive parents themselves and more likely to engage in street crime (Widom, 1989b). Cathy Widom (1989a) conducted a study of the criminal records of 667 adults who were processed in the courts twenty years earlier as abuse or neglect cases. She compared their criminal record to a matched control group that did not suffer from abuse or neglect. She concluded:

Early childhood victimization has demonstrated long-term consequences for delinquency, adult criminality, and violent criminal behavior. These results provide strong support for the cycle of violence hypothesis. . . The experience of child abuse and neglect has a substantial impact even on individuals with otherwise little likelihood of engaging in officially recorded criminal behavior . . . In a direct test of the violence-breeds-violence hypothesis, physical abuse as a child led significantly to later violent criminal behavior when other relevant demographic variables such as age, sex, and race were held constant . . . These findings indicate that abused and neglected children have significantly greater risk of becoming delinquents, criminals, and violent criminals.

Although Widom examined those at the extreme end of the corporal punishment continuum, physical abuse, it is reasonable to assume that if lots of corporal punishment leads to very poor behavioral outcomes, then moderate amounts of corporal punishment should result in moderately poor behavior. It is incumbent on those who claim corporal punishment does not contribute to aggression to prove that the demonstrable effects of harsh corporal punishment somehow evaporate when it comes to using milder amounts of physical punishment on children. It would be equivalent to someone saying, "Research may show that spending eight hours in the sun unprotected causes the skin to blister, but I believe that spending two hours in the sun has no adverse effect on the skin." There are ample research findings that sub-abusive violence against children has lasting deleterious behavioral effects (Straus, 2000).

The more a child is spanked, or otherwise physically or psychologically assaulted, the greater the number and severity of the adverse side effects of punishment will be manifested in his behavior. Likewise the fewer and milder the spankings a child receives, the milder will be the adverse side effects. This logically results in a conclusion opposite the adage, "If one is good and two is better, then I'll take three." Cautious parents should be thinking, "If a lot of spanking is bad, and a little is better, then I'll take the best situation—no spanking at all."

Murray Straus, PhD, a sociologist and co-director of the Family Research Lab at the University of New Hampshire, has been studying corporal punishment in the family for over 20 years. He found that children whose parents used corporal punishment were twice as likely to assault their siblings as children and more than twice as likely to hit their spouses in adulthood (Straus, 1983). Straus (1994) also found that the more school personnel were authorized to use corporal punishment, the higher the student assault rate was in the school. This finding also suggests that the punished students may retaliate against the school with some aggression of their own in the form of school vandalism. This relationship between officially condoned violence and the degree of violence exhibited by the public also holds true with countries. The more a nation approves of violence, the higher the infant homicide rate (Burns & Straus, 1987) and the more favorable the attitudes toward corporal punishment in a nation, the more adult violence and other crime exists (Straus, 1996). Cross-cultural studies provide additional evidence of the link between physically punitive parenting and violence. The cultures with the highest crime rates invariably emphasize the use of corporal punishment in their socialization practices (Whiting, 1963). Norris's (1989) finding that virtually all serial killers received harsh physical discipline as children is not very surprising. One culture, which is practically crime-free, uses virtually no severe forms of parental punishment (Sollenberger, 1968).

One clear path to the aggressive response created with additive punishment is that it creates a desire to retaliate. Classic examples are the intergenerational feuds of such families as the Hatfields and McCoys, gang shootings, and news items of children who murder their abusive parents. Even Saddam Hussein tried to retaliate against past-President George Bush in 1993 for the punishing bombardment of Baghdad, by training a gang of terrorists to assassinate Bush.

Philip Greven (1990) writes in his book *Spare the Child*, "Physical punishment of children consistently appears as one of the major influences shaping subsequent aggressiveness and delinquency of males (Wilson & Herrnstein, 1986)." The psychologists Ronald Slaby and Wendy Roedell in *The Development and Regulation of Aggression in Young Children* note that "one of the most reliable predictors of children's level of aggression is the heavy use by parents of harsh, punitive discipline and physical punishment." They add that "Parental punitiveness has been found to be positively correlated with children's aggression in over twenty-five studies." Children who receive harsh physical discipline from their parents are more likely to engage in juvenile delinquent behavior (Welsh, 1976).

The best evidence that violence begets violence is that over 90% of American parents spank their children (Graziano & Namaste, 1990). Why? It is certainly not good for the kids as amply demonstrated by behavioral scientists. There is little or no research data available that supports the use of violence to discipline children, and it certainly is not logical to hit a child in order to teach him not to hit other children. So why do parents continue to hit their children? The answer is simple. Parents hit their children because their parents hit them! This is the best evidence that violence begets violence. Parents are repeating the cycle of violence against their children because it was taught to them by their own parents. John Bradshaw (1988) called this process *poisonous pedagogy*. "As adults, people act the same way their parents acted *in an attempt to prove that their parents behaved correctly toward them, i.e., really loved them and really did it for their own good*." (p. 68). Research repeatedly finds that those who were spanked as children approve of corporal punishment and intend to use it on their own children (Bryan & Freed, 1982; Durrant, 1994; Graziano & Namaste, 1990; Straus & Moynihan, 1994). Moreover, those adults who were exposed to corporal punishment in childhood are more likely to behave violently toward their spouse (Straus, 1983; Straus, Gelles, & Steinmetz, 1980; Straus & Moynihan, 1994).

I am reminded of an incident I witnessed that illustrates

very clearly how children learn to behave violently from their parents. When my oldest child was a preschooler and first began playing with other children, they would regularly hit him when problems arose while playing, most likely because they were imitating their parents' behavioral problem-solving style. I taught my son that there are a number of superior ways to deal with this type of playmate misbehavior other than hitting back. One way we taught him to deal with repeated hittings, if warnings were not heeded, was to go knock on the door of the offender's parents (we lived in a condo and all the doors were in close proximity) and tell them that their child would not stop hitting. On one particular occasion I observed him do this as I gazed out our front window to where he was playing. To my amazement, I saw the parent, whom he had just reported to, storm out of her unit, stomp up to her little boy, smack him across the face and scream, "I told you not to hit!"

Chapter 3

Spanking and Your Child's Personality

Spanking adversely affects children's personality in a number of ways. It lowers self-esteem, fosters alienation, depression, and masochism, and reduces creativity and initiative. I think virtually all parents would agree that these personality outcomes are not what they desire for their children, yet by spanking them, they are increasing the probability that they will create the exact opposite personality traits in their children than what they want! The following undesirable side effects of spanking, which I have numbered as 2 through 12, are included in this chapter because they all deal with various aspects of one's personality.

Undesirable Side Effect of Spanking #2

Spanking lowers the self-esteem of children

Let's examine self-esteem first since many personality psychologists have called it the most important of all the personality traits. This is because low self-esteem interferes with the ability to genuinely love, like, or accept other people (Baron, 1974). Self-esteem refers to how worthwhile, overall, an individual believes he is as a person, that is, the belief that one is generally a good person or a bad person. Personality studies have shown that people who are higher in self-esteem are less likely to be depressed (Battle, 1987), lonely (Joubert, 1990), or shy (Zimbardo, 1977), and they are more likely to be creative (Coopersmith, 1967), popular (Simon, 1972), and take chances in games (Coopersmith, 1967). Since all these important aspects of life have been shown to be a function of self-esteem, then creating high self-esteem in children should be a key goal in parenting. Unfortunately, spanking interferes with achieving this parenting goal. Spanking lowers children's self-esteem. Hyman and Barrish (1996) surveyed 205 college freshmen. They found that those freshmen who had childhood memories of severe beatings had lower self-esteem, and were more unhappy than those who had mild and infrequent spankings.

Children who are struck by their parents are being sent a message that they are of little value. This implicit message is derived when kids see how parents normally behave in regard to those things they highly value such as certain prized possessions. Take an award-winning show car for instance—one that has twenty coats of polished lacquer and practically shines with the brilliance of a neon light. Woe to any person who dings, scratches, scuffs, or even gets a fingerprint on that kind of prize-winning finish! Kids can see that we protect from harm anything that we value highly. By inference then, if we strike and damage the "finish" on our children, their bodies, then we are sending them a clear message: "I'm not worried about damaging you. You're not as valuable as my mint condition '57 Chevy. You're only a piece of junk that doesn't need to be protected, like the old pickup in back that I let get banged up because I only use it to haul trash to the dump."

At this point some parents may be tempted to substitute yelling for spanking in order to avoid damaging their child's self-esteem. Unfortunately, this is not a good idea, either. Behavioral research shows that when verbal reprimands take the form of harsh criticism, it also lowers a child's self-esteem and erodes any sense of competence (Bandura, 1986). Name calling and put-downs may not be physical punishment, but they are a type of punishment nevertheless, because hurtful words are painful. Words are powerful and can result in as much, or more, psychological damage as physical blows. Punishment not only hurts one's self-esteem, but it also hurts feelings.

Undesirable Side Effect of Spanking #3

Spanking creates negative affect (the display of bad feelings) in children

Studies indicate that children who are hit suffer from inordinate amounts of psychological distress and depression. The fact that abused children exhibit a greater prevalence of problems such as emotional disturbance, poorer cognitive maturity, poorer interpersonal skills, lower self-esteem, greater hopelessness, are less ambitious, and have fewer friends, is well-established (Allen & Tarnowsky, 1989; Haskett & Kistner, 1991; Kirby et al., 1993; Kurtz et al., 1993; Oates et al., 1985; and Salzinger et al., 1993). The next question arises: Is there any evidence that children who receive regular corporal punishment suffer adverse emotional effects? The answer is yes, they do.

Family therapists call the confusion that children experience when they receive contradictory messages from their parents a *double-bind*. Hitting children is a classic double-bind situation because parents, who supposedly love their children, are deliberately hurting them. They sometimes even tacitly state this inherent contradiction, "I'm spanking you because I love you." Kingsley (1969) found that those exposed to double-bind situations experienced more anxiety and confusion. The discrepancy between the verbal and non-verbal information being conveyed is a sign of poor communication and dysfunctional family interactions (Bateson, 1969).

Turner and Finkelhor (1996) examined the amount of psychological distress experienced by four groups of children, those who were exposed to frequent, moderate, low, and no corporal punishment. Psychological distress in their nationally representative sample of 1042 boys and 958 girls was measured by asking the children in the study "how often in the past month they were sad, felt alone, felt bad about school, felt bad about their looks, or felt they were doing things wrong." They found that the amount of distress was significantly related to the degree of physical punishment, independent of the children's age, gender, family income, and presence of abuse.

Another study examined the effect of corporal punishment on adolescents from a nationally representative sample of 2,149 adults who were a part of the 1985 National Family Violence Survey (Straus & Kantor, 1994). The researchers found about half of the study participants reported having been hit by a parent in their adolescent years. These adults had a greater degree of depression than those who did not report being corporally punished by their parents as teenagers. In addition, the researchers found that increasing amounts of corporal punishment was associated with a greater probability of alcohol abuse, suicidal thoughts, abusing one's own children, and wife assault during adulthood.

Straus and Kantor conclude, as a result of these findings, that corporal punishment is never appropriate and, if eliminated as a discipline technique, would reduce the incidence of these societal problems. These results were replicated by a more recent study conducted in Canada. McMillan et al. (1999) surveyed 4,888 adults in Ontario. She asked them how much they had been spanked as children and then assessed their degree of anxiety, depression, and antisocial behavior. Results indicated that those who were spanked as children were more likely to develop disorders such as anxiety, depression, and a drug or alcohol problem. These results reveal that these children not only received punishment in childhood, they were punished for life.

Bachar et al. (1997) examined 871 normal Israeli high school students. They measured the students' psychiatric symptoms, emotional distress, and subjective well-being. They also measured the subjective degree of bonding the students felt with their parents, and how severe was the degree of physical punishment their parents used on them. They found that the degree of bonding had no effect on the students' emotional states. The only factor that influenced how they felt was how much corporal punishment they experienced at the hands of their parents. The more physical punishment, the higher the reported levels of emotional distress and the lower their level of reported well-being. The more corporal punishment experienced as children, the greater was the chance of being depressed in adulthood regardless of whether or not the parents were violent to each other (Straus, 1994). Punishment not only risks bad feelings, but it also erodes the emotional bonds between family members.

Undesirable Side Effect of Spanking #4

Spanking alienates the child from the parents

The best way to get a sense of this feeling of alienation toward a source of punishment is to recall the feeling you had inside the last time you were followed closely by a police cruiser while driving in traffic. If you are like most people, you had a very uncomfortable feeling. When this happens to me, I nervously watch the cruiser in my rear view mirror. The more closely the cruiser follows and the longer it shadows me, the more nervous I get. I ruminate in a panic, "Did I completely stop for that last stop sign? Did I change lanes properly? Was I late on that last red light? Was I driving over the speed limit?" I can't wait until the cruiser decides to pass me and when it does so I have a feeling of great relief. The relief is, "Whew, I didn't break a traffic law after all and I'm not going to get a ticket." The reason we feel this way toward the police car when it follows closely is because we have been punished by the police in similar situations in the past by being issued a traffic ticket.

Children who are punished try to escape the punishing environment by running away from those who supervise them (McCord, 1996). Examples are students who hide in the school restroom to smoke, teenagers who run away from home to avoid punishment, and pets who run from their owners when called. We had a neighbor once who hit his dog each time it escaped from the backyard. Eventually, the dog would not come when called. It would run and hide from the neighbor each time he called to it while trying to retrieve it. Would you rather your child love or fear you?

Dr. Gerald Patterson (1982a), a clinical psychologist with the Oregon Research Institute, found that when family members quit using physical and verbal punishment as a means of relating, their feelings toward each other change. Many children interpret physical punishment as a form of care-taker rejection (Rohner & Bourque, 1966). When family members learn non-punishing ways of interacting, they find that they begin to genuinely enjoy each other and their bonds of love and attachment grow accordingly.

Physical punishment increases the feelings of resentment toward the parents (Graziano & Namaste, 1990). It can also undermine the bonding and attachment process between the parent and child (Straus & Hill, 1997). Straus and Donnelly

(1993) found that half of all adolescents are hit by their parents. They make the sensational claim that the only way children can escape the risk of physical assault is to leave home for college or to establish their own households.

There is a paradoxical effect that takes place when the level of physical punishment crosses the threshold into severe child abuse. Abused children can display strong attachments to their abusing parents. This is called "traumatic bonding" (Painter & Dutton, 1981). This is not an isolated phenomenon. It appears to occur in a number of other human contexts involving abuse. Hostages have been found to identify with their captors and express sympathy for their cause. This became apparent to the world during a highly publicized plane hijacking in that occurred in the 1970s in Stockholm, Sweden, subsequently known as the "Stockholm Syndrome."

Social service agencies and the legal system become exasperated when battered women repeatedly refuse to extricate themselves from their abusive husbands or chronically return to them "because I love him." Counterintuitively, abuse can, and often does, create strong emotional ties between the abuser and victim. Painter and Dutton (1981) offer possible explanations: The power imbalance creates a negative self-appraisal of the person in the lower-power position, making her feel too incompetent to exist independently, and therefore more in need of the high-power person. The researchers note that the alternation between abuse and reinforcement on the part of the abuser in the relationship results in a partial schedule of reinforcement. When the reinforcing friendly contact is interspersed with physical punishment, the degree of emotional bonding becomes greatest (Fisher, 1955). It should be clear that it is not a good idea to counter the alienating effects of corporal punishment through the use of physical abuse. Creating pathological bonding is not a good cure for the alienating effects of corporal punishment. The next undesirable side effect involves the loss of children's natural spontaneity.

Undesirable Side Effect of Spanking #5

Spanking suppresses children's behavior

Punishment can suppress many behaviors besides the punished one. A child who is regularly and severely punished can overgeneralize the association between punishment and a particular act to include many other behaviors, including desirable ones. They will also then disappear along with the punished behaviors. Punishment has a generalized inhibiting effect. Laboratory rats will simply freeze up when punished. Similarly, children who are frequently punished may become inhibited, less active than other children, and withdrawn (Kandel, 1990). For instance, repeated spankings for "talking back" may lead your child to quit talking to you altogether. Criticism is a type of punishment. I'm sure most parents have seen the youth sports coach who constantly criticizes his players for mistakes. This often has the effect of turning the kids off to the game. Some may abandon the sport altogether and never return.

Even events not directly related to the punished behavior may have an inhibiting effect due to the concept called *stimulus generalization*. That is, anything that is similar to, associated with, or reminds one of an incident in which he was punished, will lead to suppression of the punished behavior. For example, a boy who is severely punished for aggression may also become passive by giving up assertiveness along with the fighting (Bandura, 1969; 1986). Another example would be a girl who is punished for telling lies may also stop sharing her fantasies with her parents. A boy who is spanked for teasing his sister may come to avoid almost all contact with her. Anything that is associated with the punishment can trigger a maladaptive avoidance response by the child in an attempt to avoid future punishment. The child may choose to avoid contact with the parents as much as possible or even curtail his routine activities for fear that he may accidentally do something that will trigger new punishment. All of these suppression effects are maladaptive responses that may result from the use of punishment. People engage in this type of inappropriate behavior for a very good reason. Logically, it serves to protect them from future punishment, but unfortunately, it is not what the punisher expected or desired. Parents often get more than they bargained for by relying on punishment to control behavior.

Carl Rogers (1954), the eminent humanistic psychologist, hypothesized that children will develop their creative potential more if they are raised in an atmosphere of psychological safety and freedom. Jack Block, in a ten-year-long longitudinal study of children, found empirical support for Rogers' hypothesis (Harrington, Block, & Block, 1987). The children of authoritarian parents, those who emphasize criticism, scorn, and harsh physical punishment as the primary means of behavior control, were less creative than the children of parents who provided a more supportive environment that emphasized reinforcement as a means of controlling their children's behavior. This indicates that not only does corporal punishment suppress the range of exploratory behaviors in children and personality characteristics such as assertiveness, but it also can suppress potential behaviors by limiting a child's ability to be creative.

The use of corporal punishment is most often equated with strict parenting, while using nonphysical alternatives is paired with the dreaded word "permissive," which has strong connotations of being bad due to the belief that the children will grow up being spoiled and out of control. In an attempt to avoid this scenario, many parents are determined to raise their children with strict discipline techniques, the cornerstone of which is spanking. Watson (1957) put this assumption to the test. He could not find any children from "very permissive" homes, so he had to conduct his study by comparing the thirty-four children from "fairly permissive" homes to the forty-seven children who were raised strictly. The permissively raised children were superior by community standards. They were more independent, had more initiative, were more cooperative, were better able to persist in the face of frustration, expressed more positive feelings about others, were less hostile, and were more creative, spontaneous, and original in their thinking. Why this counterintuitive outcome? Because parents who tightly control their children have not allowed them the freedom to live and learn responsibility that stems from self-control versus the conformity to the demands of others. Parents who rely heavily upon the force of physical threat to control their children, rather than upon the bonds of affection, risk creating children who only care about themselves and lack the capacity for sensitivity toward others.

Undesirable Side Effect of Spanking #6

Spanking contributes to antisocial behavior

The primary characteristic of the antisocial individual is lack of empathy for others. Sociopaths are only concerned about themselves and they will trample on the rights of others to satisfy their own needs. They believe in a cruel world, that everyone is out for themselves. The object becomes to take advantage of others before they get the best of you. It's an authoritarian world where might makes right (Samenow, 1984). The top dog rules because he has the most power and instills obedience by force of threat and intimidation. Man, oh man, how the antisocial personality longs to rule others in this kind of world. He's learned that one is either the ruler or victim. If others control you, you're done for. Obey, or be hit. He'll do whatever it takes to claw his way to the top of the totem pole. That's the only safe place to be. Control others—if they control you, you're going to be hurt. Punishment fosters this antisocial world view because a child learns that others are cruel—they hurt children. These others are not detached strangers—they are parents. If one's parents are cruel, imagine how bad strangers must be! The focus of social interaction becomes saving oneself from the pain inflicted by others, rather than on a social structure that is kind, gentle, guiding, and respects the dignity of human flesh. If you don't do what I say right now, WHACK! Can you imagine the fear instilled in a two-year-old who is small, weak, and relatively helpless against the powerful giants who rule the world with intimidation? Physical punishment sends the implicit message to the child that the primary motive for behaving is to avoid getting hurt. The focus of attention is on oneself. I need to behave in a way that keeps myself from receiving negative consequences as opposed to behaving in a manner that has positive conse-quences for others. Internal self-control and self-direction are sacrificed for the sake of external control by force and coercion. Instead of fostering an inner-directed conscience for doing what is right, an outer-directed fear-of-getting-caught-for-doing-wrong is developed with spanking. This created an externally-driven child who believes that being bad, or good by inference, only counts if someone finds out. This is why it is difficult to teach children to be considerate of others if punish-ment is used (McCord, 1996). Typical antisocial behaviors are cheating, lying, cruelty to others, lack of remorse, deliberately breaking things, disobedience, and difficulty getting along with others. These are the very same behaviors that characterized the children of parents who spanked (Straus, 1996). The warmth and cognitive stimulation provided to the children by their parents were not enough to overcome these antisocial effects of corporal punishment.

Egocentrism is a term coined by the late eminent developmental psychologist, Jean Piaget. He developed clever developmental tasks that illustrated how differently children think compared to adults. They are more egocentric and concrete in their thinking (Piaget, 1973) . Egocentrism refers to the fact that children cannot take another's perspective in life; they believe everyone is experiencing the world exactly as they do. That is why a young girl, when taken Christmas shopping by her father to buy something for mommy, will select a Barbie doll to give to her mother for Christmas. If she wants a doll for Christmas, then she believes everyone else is thinking and feeling exactly what she is. When adults behave this way we call them *self-centered.*

Kohlberg collected data on the development of moral intelligence. His resultant theory has four stages that range from the most primitive to the most highly-developed level of moral reasoning (Kohlberg, 1964). He states that the most primitive motive for doing what is right is the fear of punishment. The most highly-developed sense of morality is guided by one's inner principles. The use of physical punishment has been found to impede the process of moral development (Straus & Donnelly, 1993).

Ginot (1965) has an interesting perspective: "One of the worst side effects of physical punishment is that it may interfere with the development of a child's conscience. Spanking relieves guilt too easily: the child, having paid for his misbehavior, feels free to repeat it. Children develop what Selma Fraiberg (1968) calls a "'bookkeeping approach' to misconduct:

it permits them to misbehave, and thus go into debt on one side of the ledger, and pay it off in weekly installments with punishment (p. 125)." Can the negative side effects of spanking spill into the bedroom? Unfortunately, the answer is "yes."

Undesirable Side Effect of Spanking #7

Spanking creates masochistic tendencies in children

Whenever I lecture about the unintended adverse side effects of using corporal punishment on children, audience members respond with the most surprise when I mention masochism. The connection between corporal punishment and masochism is not obvious to the casual observer. However, with a little understanding of the fundamental laws of learning, the connection between sex and violence does not seem so surprising at all. Ivan Pavlov, a Nobel Prize-winning Russian physiologist-turned-psychologist, discovered the law of classical conditioning around the turn of the century. This type of learning involves a simple paired association between a reflex and a stimulus in the environment, which simply means that an animal or a person can easily be trained to have an uncontrollable emotional or movement response to anything—like desire as a response to pain. Here's how it works: Practically everyone has heard about how Pavlov conditioned his dog to salivate to a bell. What actually happened is that Pavlov discovered, during his research on salivation, that his dog would begin to salivate when it heard the research assistant open and close the lab door, even before it could see whether he was carrying dog food. What Pavlov eventually came to realize, through further experimentation, is that the dog acquired a learned connection (paired association) between the sound of the door and subsequent appearance of the food. Previous to the occurrence of these two events together (door and food), the dog did not salivate to the sound of a door (or bell as Pavlov later used for the purpose of greater experimental control). It was neutral with respect to salivation. If you watch your own animals carefully, you can see them respond to this type of learned connection in your own home. Your dog or cat will become very excited (the uncontrollable emotional response that occurs simultaneously) by any stimulus that you regularly repeat just before feeding time, such as driving up in the car, opening the cupboard door, or the sound of the can opener. As a matter of fact, you, yourself, have been conditioned to respond with similarly good, even joyous emotional responses to previously neutral events through past classical conditioning paired-association experiences, many that you likely cannot remember. Typical conditioned positive emotional responses are the joyous feelings of good will in response to Christmas symbols, positive feelings elicited by hearing certain songs popular during adolescence, and having a strong positive feeling of liking someone you just met for the first time. All of these positive feelings are triggered because they are associated with events that occurred long ago in our lives. The reason we still have powerful emotional reactions to current stimuli that are similar to those from our past is that the learning that occurs through classical conditioning is very persistent, often lasting a lifetime (Hoffman and Flesler, 1963).

How does all of this relate to masochism? Quite simply, it happens when parents show their children affection after spanking them. At these times they are unwittingly conditioning their children to associate love with pain. They are creating masochistic tendencies in their children. Why, might you ask, would parents hit their children and then follow it up with affection? It's easy to do. Many times parents who use corporal punishment fall into the trap of striking their kids too hard by accident or out of frustration and anger. When they do, they are usually horrified and quickly revert to damage control by scooping up the child and profusely apologizing with hugs and kisses and statements of "I'm sorry, you know I really love you and didn't mean to hurt you," partly to assuage their own feelings of guilt. As a matter of fact, the association between love and pain can occur without the parents showing any overt affection at all. That's because the child's pain, resulting from the corporal punishment, is always paired with feelings of love and affection—children carry these bonds of affection for their parents with them at virtually all times.

If this is true, then you would expect most people to acquire masochistic tendencies, since most children love their parents, and most parents spank their children. Unfortunately, that's exactly what we find. Straus (1994) found that 61% of college students reported they were sexually aroused when they imagined or did one of three activities in the Masochistic Sex Index: being restrained, being physically rough, or being spanked. Alfred Kinsey (1948), in his groundbreaking study of sexual behavior half a century ago, also found that more than half the people he studied were sexually aroused by a single masochistic activity—biting. Judging by all the sexually-oriented websites that spring up on the computer when one types the key word "spanking" into a web-search engine, spanking certainly appears to now reign supreme as the most popular form of masochistic sex play! As a reader told it in a letter to the *Journal of Sex Research* (1987):

> I read with keen interest your recent interview in Debonnair during your visit to India. Especially I read about the man who wanted his behind smacked for achieving orgasm. During my schoolhood in a Christian missionary Anglo-Indian Institute in Calcutta we were (all boys) often caned on our upturned, upraised buttocks by the

headmaster (with his attractive wife sometimes looking on and passing humiliating, sarcastic comments). Needless to say, this brutalized our love-maps and in certain cases brought about orgasms and a sickening addiction to the rod and a good whipping. I was nine when the canings began, and seventeen when I left school. For the others it may have started earlier, slightly. I got sexual feelings from around the age twelve, especially if she was watching. We usually collected five or six cuts of the cane, but once I got eighteen. This addiction has resulted in certain friends hiring Anglo-Indian prostitutes to spank them. One is going through a divorce because his wife can't stand an emotional, sexual cripple pervert, and leper (her words, not mine)! I brooded on this problem for a long time and have hit upon a perfect solution—self whipping! . . . (pp. 273-274).

Reprinted with permission of the Journal of Sex Research.

Additional points are made by Tom Johnson (1996) in a pamphlet titled *The Sexual Dangers of Spanking Children.* Following are excerpts:

Spanking trespasses on one of the body's most private and sexual areas—the buttocks. To fully address the wrongness of spanking children, therefore, we must consider not only the issue of physical violence, but also the issue of sexual trespass. While the harm of spanking's physical violence has been thoroughly explained and demonstrated over the past century in a vast body of academic literature, scientific research, legal treatises, and relatively recently in the popular media, it is quite rare that the sexual consequences of spanking are openly and seriously discussed.

The arguments raised herein apply equally to paddling, switching, caning, strapping, or any other mode of forcible buttock-beating. Like women's breasts, the buttocks are a sexual or erogenous part of the human anatomy, even though they are not actually sex organs. This is why baring one's buttocks in public is considered indecent as well as unlawful and why their exposure in movies or on television constitutes nudity. It is also why someone who uninvitedly fondles another person's buttocks is treated by law as a sexual offender. The sexual nature of the buttocks is explained not only by their proximity to the genitals, but also by their high concentration of nerve endings which lead directly to sexual nerve centers. Hence, the buttocks are a major locus of sexual signals.

We do children a disservice if we fail to recognize that they too have erogenous zones which deserve consideration and respect. We generally understand that fondling or caressing a child's buttocks is a sexual offense. The question, then, is why slapping a child's buttocks is not considered a sexual offense? A plausible explanation for this breach of logic is simply that the majority of people are unable or unwilling to believe there could be anything indecent about a practice as old, common and accepted as the spanking of children—something which nearly everyone has received, given or witnessed at least once. And since spankings typically come from esteemed or even beloved authority figures, many people are loath to question this behavior. Freedom from sexual violation is one of the basic tenets of liberty most revered by Americans. As this principle of inviolacy applies to adults, it should apply equally, if not especially, to children, who are below the age of consent.

As in ages past, there are people today who are sexually excited by spanking. This trait, which is often expressed in pornography and associated with sadomasochism, is known in the scientific literature as flagellantism. While many flagellants seek to engage in consensual spanking between adults, some find the spanking of minors to be either more arousing or more opportune. Since children in this country up to eighteen years old can still be legally and forcibly spanked by parents, guardians, teachers, school principals and other child care professionals, it is often easy for flagellants to obtain positions where they can sexually abuse children with little or no fear of repercussions.

History, court records and current events contain numerous cases of flagellant sexual abuse against defense-less victims, and there is no telling how many instances have gone unreported. Even without sexual motives on the part of the punisher, spanking can interfere with a child's normal sexual and psychological development. Because the buttocks are so close to the genitals and so multiply linked to sexual nerve centers, slapping them can trigger powerful and involuntary sensations of sexual pleasure. This can happen even in very young children, and even in spite of great, clearly-upsetting pain.

This kind of sexual stimulation, which undermines any disciplinary purpose and which most people would agree is unsuitable for children in any context, can cause a child to impressionably attach his or her sexuality to the idea of spanking. This fixation may endure to cause problems in adult life. Or, on the other hand, the child might react against these unseemly feelings of pleasure by repressing his or her sexuality, so much perhaps that as an adult, he or she has difficulty experiencing sexual pleasure and inti-macy.

An additional danger is that the confusing mixture of pleasure with pain will become the basis for permanent sadomasochistic tendencies. Sadomasochism, in which a person takes pleasure in inflicting or receiving pain, drives behavior that is destructive to oneself and to others, and therefore to society at large. While the intensity and background of individuals' sadomasochism varies widely, the great majority of studied cases point to a single origin: childhood whippings, usually on the buttocks.

The odds that spanking a child will lead to psychosexual aberrations would be difficult to calculate. However, the fact that there is any chance at all of these serious problems occurring should be reason enough to do away with the practice of spanking. The risks are completely unnecessary.

Spanking can seriously injure a child's sense of modesty. Consequently, the child whose buttocks are slapped may experience deep and lasting sexual shame, especially if the punishment is done in front of others or involves a state of undress. Actually, there are some adults who consciously emphasize this humiliation as part of the punishment (and some, for that matter, who do not limit spanking to younger children or even to preteens). But just as inflicting sexual shame is an unthinkable punishment for adults in any civilized society, it is surely an outrageous way to treat children.

It is a strange inconsistency, furthermore, for adults to exhort children to modesty while punishing them in a way that aggressively denies their modesty and privacy. Such mixed messages tend to confuse children or make them skeptical toward adult authority. Especially if adults hope to instill children with strong values of modesty, self-respect, and respect for others—values that become very important through the trials of puberty and adolescence—adults should teach by example and refrain from the disrespectful practice of bottom-slapping. Society has failed to squarely address the serious implications of spanking's punitive/sexual duality.

As long as paddeling is legal, it will be abused. For example, it was reported in *The Sacramento Bee* (1995) that a private school headmaster was arrested in Arizona on charges of forcing a 15-year-old girl to disrobe and bow down before him reciting the Lord's Prayer as he struck her with a wooden paddle. He also made her bend over, spread her legs, and grab the end of a table and submit to another swat as she cried. The teenager's mother witnessed the paddeling but said she was too frightened to stop it. Her daughter was left with bruises and welts on her buttocks as a result of the swats.

Her young sister heard her cries for help while she was waiting in the next room. All this happened even though the girl was not a student at the school. The teen and her mother were there only to consider enrollment at the school.

The headmaster reportedly told the girl during her long ordeal that she needed to understand corporal punishment, a method of discipline used at the school. The headmaster had been accused of child abuse before. He faced trial for allegedly bruising the buttocks of a 9-year-old student in another paddling incident at the school.

Arizona law permits authorities and parents to paddle children with appropriate force. Parents in favor of corporal punishment rallied in support of the headmaster. They said they enrolled their children at the academy because they wanted stricter discipline.

Although spanking teaches us some unintended lessons about sex, it can interfere with learning about the rest of the world.

Undesirable Side Effect of Spanking #8

Spanking interferes with children's learning and achievement

Children who are frequently punished by their teachers come to hate school. School dropouts stay away from school due to the intense dislike and avoidance of the punisher and situation in which it occurred (Bandura, 1986). The negative emotions elicited by spanking, such as fear, anger, and frustration, are incompatible with learning. People simply do not learn as well while in these emotional states. This makes it difficult or nearly impossible to teach the child who was spanked what he did wrong and what the teacher, or parent, would like him to do instead. Children who are spanked perform more poorly in school compared to children who are not (Straus & Mathur, 1995; Straus & Paschall, 1998). B. F. Skinner (1972) wrote, "Punitive measures, whether administered by police, teachers, spouses, or parents, have well-known standard effects: (1) escape—education has its own name for that: truancy, (2) counterattack—vandalism on schools and attacks on the teachers, (3) apathy—a sullen do-nothing withdrawal. The more violent the punishment, the more serious the by-products" (p. 26).

Being subjected to physical punishment as a child is correlated with reduced occupational achievement (Straus & Gimpel, 1992; Straus, 1994). Those who were physically punished are also are less likely to graduate from college, even after experimenters controlled for parents' education and income levels (Straus & Mathur, 1995). There are at least four reasons for this: Physically punished children do not learn good interpersonal skills, which are highly valued in the workplace—they are probably more aggressive and less cooperative; they carry their emotional baggage with them, from their childhood discipline experiences, into their occupations and find it more difficult to perform; they did not learn as much in school and have fewer skills; and finally, they might have less intelligence. Carrey (1995) found that children who were physically abused had an average IQ of 88 compared to 101 in the nonabused group. Does sub-abusive physical punishment lower intelligence too? According to recent research, the answer is yes (Straus & Paschall, 1998). The more corporal punishment experienced by children examined in the study, aged two to nine, the lower their scores on a test of cognitive ability fell over a four-year period while the cognitive ability scores of those who were not spanked increased over the same period. He concluded that corporal punishment retards the rate of children's cognitive development. The explanation may lie in the different attitudes behind parents who hit and those who do not. A punitive parent who believes children should be seen and not heard and demands blind obedience backed up with the fear of being struck, is less likely to promote cognitive development through explaining and reasoning with children, and by stifling exploration and creativity in the child. The results of Straus's research were reported in the media by Reuters (1998):

> WASHINGTON (Reuters)—Children who are never spanked, or hardly ever spanked, fare better on some intelligence tests than children who are frequently smacked, researchers say.
>
> It could be because parents who do not spank their children spend more time talking to them and reasoning with them, the researchers said.
>
> "Some parents think this is a waste of time, but research shows that such verbal parent-child interactions enhance the child's cognitive ability," Murray Straus of the University of New Hampshire, who worked on the study, said in a statement. His team studied more than 900 children who were aged 1 to 4 at the start of the trial in 1986. They were given tests of cognitive ability—which is the ability to learn and to recognize things—in 1986 and again in 1990. They then accounted for factors such as whether the father lived with the family, how many children there were in the family, how much time the mother spent with the child, ethnic group, birth weight, age and gender. They watched mothers with their children and questioned them about corporal punishment. The more the children were spanked or otherwise physically punished, the lower their scores on the test, they told the World Congress of Sociology in Montreal over the weekend. "The cognitive ability of the children who were not spanked in either of the

two sample weeks increased, and the cognitive ability of children who were frequently spanked decreased," Straus said. He said it was not a case of the spanked child losing ability, but rather not gaining it as quickly as he or she should. "The children who were spanked didn't get dumber," Straus said. "What the study showed is that spanking is associated with falling behind the average rate of cognitive development, not an absolute decrease in cognitive ability." Straus said it seemed that parents who did not hit their children reasoned more with them to control their behavior.

"We found that the less corporal punishment mothers in this sample used, the more cognitive stimulation they provided to the child," Straus said.

Straus said there was a trend against slapping and spanking children in the United States, but studies show most parents still do hit their children. He thinks there should be an education campaign. "If parents knew the risk they were exposing their children to when they spank, I am convinced millions would stop," Straus said.

Copyright Reuters Limited 2002.
Reprinted with permission of Reuters.

While spanking can interfere with general learning, unfortunately it teaches us some very specific lessons about social interactions we may not want to learn.

Undesirable Side Effect of Spanking #9

Spanking models undesirable behavior in children

We've already examined how spanking increases aggression by modeling aggressive behavior. In addition to teaching children to be aggressive, spanking sends the implicit message to children that the solution to problems in others' behavior is to hurt them. I think it is safe to assume that parents do not want their children to learn this type of lesson. This undesirable side effect of punishment is more a function of missed opportunities. If parents routinely respond to behavioral problems with violence, then that is all their children will learn. They will imitate their parents and behave likewise. If instead, parents responded to problems with others by using conflict mediation skills, communication skills, setting group goals, problem-solving skills, negotiating, accepting differences, cooperation, active listening, behavioral contracting, education, reasoning, creative solutions, participative management, and compromise, think how much more competent their children would become in dealing with life's problems! In addition, these alternatives set a positive tone. Instead of creating a negative world for the child, filled with anger or attacking, parents will be modeling a more mature world view their children filled with the positive virtues of patience, kindness, trust, cooperation, restraint, and empathy. What is the message that we would prefer our kids to hear? For most, I think it would definitely be the nonviolent alternatives. Tragically, after sending the wrong message to children about how to deal with problems in the world when they are spanked, it doesn't even accomplish the intended effect—to eliminate the undesirable behavior.

Undesirable Side Effect of Spanking #10

Spanking does not eliminate the undesirable behavior

The late B. F. Skinner, an eminent behavioral psychologist, argued that punishment does not really eliminate an undesirable behavior; rather, it suppresses the behavior when the punisher is present. The undesirable behavior is likely to reoccur in other settings where the punisher is not present or punishment is unlikely. Think about the case of teen smokers: Often they are caught smoking by school authorities or their parents and punished. Does this eliminate their smoking behavior? Not a chance. Instead they simply become more crafty at hiding their smoking. They will only light up when they are away from home or their parents are at work. *What kids really learn from punishment is how not to get caught.*

Yes, corporal punishment has the apparent advantage of abating an undesirable behavior more quickly than alternative discipline strategies (Gershoff, 2002). However, this "can hardly be called a meaningful positive outcome. A more important outcome variable would be the likelihood that the child did not repeat the same transgression over days, weeks, or even months" (Holden, 2002, p. 591).

Lovaas and Simmons (1969) demonstrated this effect in a study of self-mutilation by autistic children. One autistic boy was hitting himself about thirty times per minute. He was punished with a shock to the leg. The self-hitting immediately stopped. Was his hitting extinguished or suppressed? The answer was clear when the experimenters noticed that the boy would not hit himself only when the therapist who administered the punishment was present. In the presence of other therapists he continued to hit himself as before.

Skinner called this effect *discrimination learning.* An organism quickly learns that punishment only occurs in the presence of the punisher. Just look at people's driving behavior. Practically all drivers regularly break traffic laws when they feel it is unlikely a traffic officer will ticket the infraction, such as not coming to a complete stop at a stop sign. There is a stop sign in the middle of the block in my neighborhood. It is located on one of the out-of-the-way back streets that is infrequently traveled. I counted the number of cars that made a complete stop at the stop sign one afternoon. Only four of twenty-seven cars made a complete stop, with most of them barely even bothering to slow down for the stop sign! Of course the reason they do not stop is because they have never seen a police car on that isolated street and they know that they will not be punished for doing wrong. I suspect that only the four people who stopped for the stop sign had an internally-guided sense of right and wrong with respect to traffic laws and were not dependent on the external presence of an enforcer to do what was right. Wouldn't it be better to have a child that chose not to do something wrong based upon the internal constraints of a conscience and respect and love for her parents rather than only to avoid a painful punishment?

Focusing on punishment can serve as a positive reinforcer for undesirable behavior. If children realize the only way they can receive the adult attention they crave is by misbehaving, then they deliberately will do something wrong in order to get attention, even if the attention is in the form of punishment. A dramatic example of how powerful is the need for attention and how much pain one will endure to receive it comes from early studies of autistic children (Lovaas & Bucher, 1974). An eight-year-old boy was noted to hit himself 2,700 times in ninety minutes after caretakers inadvertently had trained him to do so by reinforcing his self-destructiveness with attention. Their natural inclination was to run over to him and provide comfort in response to his acts of self-destruction. The researchers tested the hypothesis that attention was sustaining the self-harmful behavior by refraining from providing any attention to the boy when he hit himself (nonreinforcement). After only eight extinction trials (ninety-minute periods when the boy received no response from his caretakers for hitting himself), the self-hitting behavior disappeared entirely. Ironically, not only does spanking fail to eliminate undesired behavior, but there is evidence that it can increase the occurrence of the very behaviors it is trying to stop!

Undesirable Side Effect of Spanking # 11

Children are more likely to engage in the forbidden behavior

Punishment can serve as a powerful incentive to increase

the attraction of forbidden acts. Just look at the attraction that smoking holds for teenagers. Before the addiction takes hold, it is not the appeal of coughing and hacking upon inhaling the first cigarette that sustains their smoking. It is the actual and threatened punishment of parents and school authorities that makes them persist past the early aversion to inhaling to eventually become addicted. *Psychological reactance* is a term used by psychologists that refers to people's tendency to do the opposite of what they are told to do when they feel their freedom of choice is being threatened. The classic example of psychological reactance is the teenage daughter who is forbidden by her parents to see her boyfriend. As everyone knows, this will only extend the relationship by making the daughter desire her boyfriend more than ever, and more than likely, be anxious to defy her parents by continuing to see him. This is alternatively known as the *Romeo and Juliet* or *Forbidden Fruit* effect. Why was Romeo's desire for Juliet more important than life itself and Eve's desire to eat the apple more important than paradise? Because both were forbidden activities that carried the threat of punishment. The theory behind this type of behavior is that people are motivated to maintain their freedom of choice (Brehm, 1972). When someone threatens to take away the freedom to do something, there is only one way to prove that one still has the freedom of choice, and that is to "react" against the restriction by engaging in the forbidden behavior. So when someone is punished for doing something (which is the same as forbidding them to do it), it has the same effect as taking away one's freedom to engage in the punished activity. Then what logically follows, according to reactance theory, is that the individual is highly motivated to engage in the punished or "forbidden" behavior by engaging in it. This is what the research has found is the case. Joubert (1992) found that those college students who reported that their parents used punitive discipline styles (spanking, scolding, and verbal abuse) had higher psychological reactance scores than those students whose parents used a discipline style based on rewards such as praise. Although correlational in nature, the author hypothesized that "These results are consistent with an interpretation that the [cause] of higher degrees of psychological reactance are found in more extensive encounters with aversive control, possibly leading to the person developing traits of being "prickly" or "contrary" (p. 1115).

This line of research has implications for the authoritarian parenting style in which children are ordered to obey, "or else." Studies have found that reactance can be strongly induced in people when they learn that another merely intends to exert influence over them. Subjects who were ordered to write an essay supporting one side of an issue reacted strongly against the order. They shifted their attitudes to believe the opposite of the one proposed. Conversely, subjects' initial views did not change in the group that had received only a suggestion on what side of the issue to support (Heller, Pallak, & Picek, 1973). Imposing excessive control upon a child externally, through the use of punishment by the parent, does not encourage children to think independently, making it more difficult for them to learn self-control. In order to learn self-restraint, and acquire an internal control mechanism, alternatives to the punitive, controlling external parent figure are needed (Eisenman & Sirgo, 1991).

Another means through which psychological reactance can occur is that children whose behavior is primarily controlled through the use of punishment, rather than praise, purposefully engage in the undesired behavior because they are starved for attention. Children crave adult attention. It is more rewarding to them than anything else in the world, so they will do practically anything to get it. This means that if they are ignored when they are doing things right (not acting up), and only get adult interaction for doing something wrong, then they will engage in the wrongful behaviors just to get adult attention, even *if it is accompanied by punishment*. A good example would be the class clown. When he is scolded or sent to the principal's office for his antics, he may not construe this as punishing. He may find that his ability to temporarily halt class activities affords him a much desired sense of power. Also, he may find it desirable and exciting to get everyone's attention by being featured in the class spotlight.

Power and Chapieski (1986) studied fourteen-month-olds who played with their mothers. They recorded what objects babies reached for and the mothers' attempts to restrain them. Physical punishment proved unsuccessful in two different ways. Those mothers who used physical punishment had babies who scored lower on a test of development, especially in spatial skills and problem solving. As far as the effectiveness of deterring children from grasping forbidden objects, the babies of mothers who physically punished them were more likely to reach for the breakable objects again and again and the least likely to obey restrictions compared to the no-or low-discipline mothers.

A related issue is the finding that punishment will increase the persistence of a behavior (Deur & Parke, 1968; Linden, 1976). The best way to get rid of an undesirable behavior is to not reinforce it (ignore it), called *nonreinforcement* by psychologists, and eventually it will disappear. However, if punishment is used in an attempt to eliminate a behavior that is being reinforced, it will take longer for it to disappear than if punishment had not been used. An example would be a child who runs into the street. This situation is always the trump card for parents who insist on using physical punishment. "I have to spank. What if my child runs into the street? Spanking can save his life!" Any parent would be very anxious to eliminate this behavior as soon as possible. However, this research indicates that spanking a child for running in the street will only prolong the amount of time the child will continue to run into the street.

"Street-running behavior" will extinguish more quickly after it ceases to be rewarding to the child if an alternative method to punishment is used. The alternative is to not punish a child with a spanking for running into the street, but to calmly carry the child back in the house or yard as a means of nonreinforcement until the rewarding aspects of street running behavior extinguish (such as satisfying the child's curiosity). If the child is old enough to understand, a simple statement should accompany removal from the street such as, "Mommy does not want you to go into the street because you could get hurt by a car." Simultaneously, the parent should reinforce a behavior incompatible with running into the street, such as playing in the yard or house. This could be accomplished by playing in the yard with the child or giving him your attention by saying periodically, "Look at how good Junior plays. He does not leave the yard. He stays away from the street and plays with his toys. Here's a (kiss, a hug, or a treat) for being a good boy." Parents would also be wise to invoke situational control by not allowing preverbal children access to dangerous traffic and to watch them more carefully. The research implications are that these alternative scenarios will be more effective in reducing the desire to run into the street than the use of punishment.

Another explanation for why punishment can increase children's desire to engage in the forbidden act is provided by *self justification theory* (cognitive dissonance) from social psychology (Festinger & Carlsmith, 1959). This theory is based upon the principle that most people are motivated to justify their own actions, beliefs, and feelings. An example would be a teenage girl who smokes. The real reason she smokes is probably because she started smoking to appear more grown up and assert her independence from her parents by "proving" that she could do whatever she wants to do. After she becomes addicted to the nicotine, she will continue to smoke even after her independence needs are no longer relevant, primarily because she is addicted and cannot quit. However, if you were to ask her why she continues to smoke, even though she knows it is bad for her health to do so, she will probably say something like: "Yeah, well, I quit a couple of times but then I gained weight each time, so now I smoke because it keeps my weight down." People are masters at rationalizing their behavior. No matter what they are doing they can find a perfectly rational and reasonable reason for doing it. Take the case of tobacco executives who profit immensely from the untimely deaths of 400,000 people in the U.S. each year. How do they justify their positions? Before their recent court setbacks, they did it by smoking themselves, and claiming that smoking was as safe as playing video games and eating twinkies.

The other half of self-justification is insufficient justification. This occurs when people are given a small reward for doing something, or a mild punishment, to stop a behavior. The way in which it works can be seen in a classic experiment by Festinger and Carlsmith (1959). They asked two groups of students to participate in an interesting experiment. What the students actually did was work boring tasks for one hour. Then the experimenters asked both groups to recruit new students by telling the new students a white lie. They were told to say the experiment would be very interesting. After their attempt to recruit the new students, half of the participants were paid one dollar each for their time and the other half were paid twenty dollars each. Finally, both groups were asked to rate how interesting they thought the tasks were in the experiment. Which group do you think rated the experiment as more interesting? If you're like most people you answered the twenty dollar group because they were paid more money to tell their white lie. But amazingly, the opposite happened. The group that was paid only one dollar rated the experiment as much more interesting. Why? It is the insufficient justification effect. They did not attribute the reason they told the prospective students the experiment was interesting to the money they were paid, because it was an insufficient amount to justify lying. They attributed the reason for saying the experiment was interesting to the fact that it must really have been interesting, or why would they say it was? But in the other group, those paid twenty dollars for lying, easily attributed their lie to the fact that they were paid handsomely for doing so. They did not have to search for a reason why they lied. The money paid to them for doing so was sufficient justification. The point of this research is that people can justify their actions in one of two ways, internally or externally. If there is a sufficient external reason for justifying actions, as in the case of the twenty dollar group, people will readily accept that it adequately explains why they behaved the way they did. When there is insufficient external justification, they will have to resort to an internal justification, such as changing their attitudes or beliefs in an attempt to explain their behavior.

What does all this have to do with corporal punishment and reactance? Simply this: When a child is given strong punishment, such as spanking, for engaging in a highly desirable behavior, such as playing with the stereo knobs, he will not touch them in the presence of the punisher. But what will happen when he is alone? He will want to touch them more than ever and will find it very difficult to refrain from doing so when there is no threat of punishment, because the punisher in not around to act as an enforcer. Why will he find the knobs so enticing? Because he will attribute his not touching them to the fact that he received harsh punishment, rather than to the fact that the knobs are not that desirable.

Now let's compare what would happen in a case where the child received mild nonphysical punishment, such as a verbal rebuke like, "Please do not touch the knobs any more. I don't like it when you touch the stereo knobs." Since only mild verbal displeasure was used, the child cannot attribute the reason for not playing with the knobs to something external, like the threat of harsh physical punishment. Therefore he must attribute the reason for not playing with the knobs to an internal source, like his attitudes or beliefs. He would likely believe that the reason he did not play with the knobs in the presence of the punisher to the fact that they are just not that much fun to play with.

I know this scenario sounds incredible but it has very strong empirical support. Here are two such experiments:

Elliott Aronson, a social psychologist at the University of California, Santa Cruz, asked five-year-olds to rate the attractiveness of several toys (Aronson & Carlsmith, 1963). Then they told each child that they could not play with the toy they rated the highest. Half the children were threatened with mild verbal punishment for not obeying ("I would be a little angry") and the other half were threatened with more severe punishment ("I would be very angry; I would have to take all of the toys and go home and never come back again"). After that, the experimenters left the room and watched the children through a one-way mirror. None of the children played with the forbidden toy. They were all able to resist the temptation. The experimenters returned to the room again and had each child rate how attractive they now found the forbidden toys. The children who were threatened with mild punishment now found that the forbidden toys were less attractive than they originally were to them. In contrast, the severely threatened group continued to rate their toys as highly desirable. Some even rated them as more desirable than they did before they were threatened. These children had a good external reason for not playing with the toy so they did not have to search for additional reasons. Therefore, they continued to like the toy. However, the mild threat group could not find an adequate external reason for not playing with the toy, and they succeeded in convincing themselves that the reason they did not play with the toy was because they really did not like it.

Jonathan Freedman (1965) supported Aronson's findings with a similar study. He put a very desirable battery-powered robot in a room full of mediocre toys. Naturally, all of the child wanted to play with the robot most. He told the children not to play with the robot and threatened half the children with mild punishment and half with severe punishment. He then left the school and never came back. Nine weeks later a woman came to the school to administer a test to the same children in the same room. They were not aware she was really there to observe their reaction to the robot toy. While the children were waiting, she casually suggested they might want to play with the toys in the room. Almost all of the mildly threatened children refused to play with the robot while almost all of the children who had been threatened with severe punishment played with the robot.

In other words, harsh punishment acts as an external reason for people to control their behavior, but only in the presence of the punisher. Their behavior control does not generalize to other times. It is not permanent. Mild punishment, such as expressing verbal displeasure, on the other hand, forces people to search for an internal reason for obeying. It generalizes to situations beyond the punisher and is more lasting. This outcome sounds a lot like what parents are really looking for. They would rather their children obey their wishes because they have incorporated it into their internal value system, rather than out of fear of physical punishment. Coerced virtue is not real and will likely only be temporary. The threat of punishment only creates the outward semblance of virtue. True virtue is not forced. It comes from within.

Thomas Gordon (1989) believes reactance is a function of control. He believes that, "When one person tries to control another, you can always expect some kind of reaction from the controllee." He says those who espouse control, power, and strong discipline parenting strategies are misguided. They assume children passively submit to power-based control without resistance and even desire it. He states it does not make them feel more secure. It is not benign and constructive. Rather than satisfying children's developmental needs, it is actually demeaning, frightening, painful, and devalues the importance of the child's needs. Children never want punitive discipline. In his Parent Effectiveness Training classes Gordon compiled a list of twenty-four different ways in which children typically react in a negative way to demands of obedience to parental authority. Many are a variation of basic reactance. They include:

"Resisting, defying, being negative;

Rebelling, disobeying, being insubordinate, sassing;

Retaliating, striking back, counterattacking, vandalizing;

Breaking rules and laws;

Throwing temper tantrums, getting angry;

Lying, deceiving, hiding the truth;

Banding together, forming alliances, organizing against the adult;

Giving up, feeling defeated, loafing, goofing off;

Leaving, escaping, staying away from home, running away, quitting school, cutting classes;

Not talking, ignoring, using the silent treatment, writing the adult off, keeping one's distance;

Getting sick, developing psychosomatic ailments;

Drinking heavily, using drugs."

He concludes that when parents rely upon punitive discipline as a means of exerting power and control, they *create the very behaviors they most dislike in their children*. In addition, they unwittingly set the stage for a constant escalation in the intensity of these punitive control tactics, which can result in serious consequences.

A reader expressed to *Dear Abby* (1995) how powerful and tragic reactance can be:

Dear Abby: I am a 47-year-old woman married to a wonderful man who is my second husband. When I read the letter in your column from the 13-year-old who was not allowed to talk to her boyfriend, it reminded me of what happened when my parents refused to let me see a boy I was in love with when I was 14. (I'll call him Ray).

Although I couldn't stop loving Ray, my parents refused to let me see or talk to him outside of school. On my 16th birthday, I again asked permission and was finally permitted to see him two or three times a week in my home, under very stressed conditions, and I was allowed a 15-minute phone call once a day.

At age 17, I ran away and married Ray, a boy I loved but didn't really know because my parents wouldn't let me spend enough time with him. After several years of sadness, we divorced. While rearing our three children, I graduated from high school and went to college.

I must tell you that my parents learned from my experience. When my sisters were 13 or 14 and fell in love, my mother talked to me. I suggested they be allowed to talk to their boyfriends on the phone and have them over for visits as long as grades, chores, sleep, etc., were not compromised.

Although my parents never left them alone with the boys, the atmosphere was relaxed. My sisters never had the need to run away and marry their young boyfriends to be with them. Predictably, they outgrew those loves and are now married to "new loves."

Parents should not be frightened by young love, and should allow their children the freedom to explore friendships in a safe environment. Of course, that takes a lot of time, love, and patience, but in the end it will pay high dividends.

WISER NOW IN PENNSYLVANIA

DEAR WISER NOW: Yours was not the only letter I received pointing out that forbidding young people to see one another will only drive them together. Your parents are to be commended for learning from your experience, and for taking your advice when dealing with your younger sisters. Thank you for writing. Your letter may help countless teens.

As seen in Dear Abby by Abigail Van Buren a.k.a. Jeanne Phillips and founded by her mother Pauline Phillips. ©Universal Press Syndicate. Reprinted with permission. All rights reserved.

Undesirable Side Effect of Spanking #12

It raises the punishment threshold

Humans have an amazing ability to adapt to routine circumstances. Sometimes this is adaptive, as when Eskimos adapt to the extreme cold. Unfortunately, the natural tendency of humans to adapt also occurs in abusive situations as well. Psychologists call this process *adaptation and habituation*. It occurs when an organism is exposed to a constant or repeating stimulus over long periods of time. After a while the stimulus loses its effect and a stronger stimulus is required to get a response. A child who is repeatedly spanked will eventually adapt to the level of punishment and become less responsive to it. Azrin and Holtz (1966) showed how this effect works with punishment by giving rats a mild shock for bar pressing. They then gradually increased the level of shock intensity. The animals adapted to each new level. It soon had no effect in suppressing their bar-pressing behavior. When the rats adapted to each level of shock, the experimenters had to increase the intensity again and again in order for it to have any effect. They found that an extreme level of shock can be administered in this fashion with surprisingly little effect on suppressing behavior. Therein lies one of the greatest dangers of using punishment to suppress behavior. One has to constantly increase the intensity for it to have the intended effect. This is the behavioral mechanism that directly feeds into child abuse. When children become accustomed to pain they build immunity to its deterrent effects (McCord, 1996). There are two reasons why the children who receive the most punishment, or are the most abused, are usually the least well-behaved. One major reason is that they end up displaying all the other unintended negative side effects of punishment, and the other reason is that they quickly adapt to the harsh levels of punishment and it loses its deterrent effect.

These children who adapt to harsh levels of punishment eventually grow up to be adults who are more likely to use harsh physical punishment on their children and spouses (Straus & Yodanis, 1995; Widom, 1989b). Their adaptation to physical punishment also makes them more likely to end up in abusive relationships (Hilberman & Munson, 1978). They have developed in a manner that comes to view physically abusive relationships as normal (Painter & Dutton, 1981).

I can just hear some parents arguing now, "How could all these things happen to a child's personality just because she got spanked? Look at me. I was spanked as a child and I turned out all right." Social psychologists tell us this is a very risky argument because we are not inclined to see our own faults. As writer William Saroyan put it, "Every man is a good man in a bad world—as he himself knows." This is called the self-serving bias. People tend to rate their behavior, personalities, and intentions more favorably than others rate them (Dunning et al., 1989; Miller & Ross, 1975). This overly favorable view of ourselves is not necessarily a bad thing. It can serve a positive function by providing a nice cognitive coping mechanism that keeps us happy with optimism and hope. People who rate themselves more realistically suffer from a clinical condition called *depressive realism* (Abramson, Metalsky, & Alloy, 1989). The point is, we don't really know how our personalities were affected by spanking. How is it possible to know what we would have been like had we not been spanked? Isn't it possible that we would be more outgoing, trusting, competent, sociable, charitable, relaxed, successful or less temperamental, passive, or aggressive—had we not been spanked?

Another way to add weight to the validity of the findings that spanking has a negative impact on children's personalities is to see if the process of eliminating spanking will reverse the damaging personality effects. Dr. Gerald Patterson (1982b), a clinical psychologist, tried this. He found that teaching parents to use nonphysical punishment reduces the degree that children exhibit depression, aggression, academic failure, and social rejection.

In conclusion, the research evidence makes it clear that spanking results in long-term emotional and psychological damage to children. This personality damage is entirely unnecessary. Using the nonphysical alternative discipline techniques to discipline children would not only eliminate the damaging psychological effects on children, but it would have the bonus effect of improving their behavior too! Each spank that we deliver adds another smudge that tarnishes the inherent sparkle of a child's personality.

Chapter 4

Spanking and Your Child's Health

The use of corporal punishment also exacts a huge toll on our children's health. In the most comprehensive report to date on child abuse, a fifteen-member board of experts, appointed by the Department of Health and Human Services, compiled statistics on child abuse deaths and injuries. It was commissioned by the United States Advisory Board on Child Abuse and Neglect. The 248-page report, entitled "A Nation's Shame: Fatal Child Abuse and Neglect in the United States" concluded that over 2,000 children are killed each year by their caretakers (Cavaliere, 1995). It found that "more preschool children are killed by their parents than die from falls, choking, suffocation, drowning or fires (p.34)." In addition, 18,000 children are permanently disabled and another 142,000 are seriously injured by their caretakers each year. These are shocking statistics. The medical cost must be hundreds of millions, not to mention the psychological cost. This is a completely unnecessary social tragedy. Many of these deaths or injuries would not occur if we did not condone corporal punishment as a society. Dr. Murray Straus, a sociologist who is the Director of the Family Research Project at the University of New Hampshire says, "Most cases of physical abuse are essentially physical punishment that's gotten out of hand."

The citizens of Sweden have determined that they will not tolerate this kind of assault on their children by passing laws that forbid the use of corporal punishment on children by anyone, including parents (Ziegert, 1983). This is a sensible step to take as a way to help reverse the cultural acceptance and condoning of corporal punishment. As the new anti-corporal-punishment attitude starts to reverse old beliefs, then the deaths and injuries ought to decline commeasurately.

Undesirable Side Effect of Spanking #13

Corporal punishment causes physical injuries

If all spanking consisted of was just a quick swat on the behind to reinforce a parent's point to the child, no physical damage would ever occur. The damage done would probably be limited to the psychological realm. Unfortunately, we live in a world that is too messy to confine spanking to this. Too many things can and do go wrong on the way to a simple, neatly pack-aged little spanking. First off, many parents are under a lot of stress and they have a lot of pent-up anger and frustration. The things that children are wont to do add to the stress levels of parents, and kids also make convenient and easy targets for venting anger. This creates a volatile mixture. First, we have a force that results from a parent who is many times stronger than a young child, then we multiply that force by adding an adrenaline rush from the anger, and finally we unleash it upon a weak and defenseless child. The outcome is what you would expect under these conditions. The parent unwittingly injures the child. This is not a rare situation. A national survey found that 80% of Canadian parents admitted having come close to losing control while disciplining their children (Straus & Mouradian, 1998) while one third of a sample of parents in two different studies spanked their children impulsively or while irritated, frustrated, and out of control (Carson, 1986; Holden & Miller, 1997). One study found that 46% of mothers admitted to having spanked their child at least once while so angry that they "lost it" (Straus & Mouradian, 1998). Estimates of the number of children that end up dying each year in the U.S. in the name of physical discipline range up to 5,000, including those recorded as "accidents" (Hutchings, 1988). One physician estimates that for every one child who dies from non-accidental head injury, four others are neurologically handicapped (MacKeith, 1974).

Contrary to the mistaken belief that the buttocks are a safe place to spank or paddle children, possible tissue damage that can result from spankings extend beyond contusions and lacerations. Hematomas, bruising of the coccyx, fracturing of the sacrum, incontinence from damage to the cauda equina nerve bundle, sciatic nerve damage, testicular hematoma, and hemorrhaging are also possible (California Medical Association, 1985). It is not medically safe to strike children's behinds!

In addition, parents who believe in corporal punishment rarely limit themselves to spanking. They also report regularly using a whole array of corporal responses including slapping, shoving, whipping, pulling hair, slugging, shaking, choking, kicking, and throwing objects (Berger, et al., 1988). Kadushin and Martin (1981) found that of the 66 child abuse cases they studied, most were an escalation of ordinary physical punishment. In response to their children's adaptation to a given level of punishment, the abusive parents increased the intensity of spanking, hitting, or shoving until abuse or injury resulted, in a desperate attempt to obtain the desired response (Marion, 1982). The parents never realized that spanking was ineffective. They were misled by the temporary effects it had on suppressing the undesirable behavior, and fell into the escalation spiral trap. The Gallup Organization conducted a survey of parents. They found that child abuse estimates are low, with actual physical child abuse cases about 16 times higher than what is officially reported to government agencies. George

Gallup, Jr., company chairman, said that the findings "will shock you. They will anger you. And they will sadden you." (USA Today, 1995.)

Tragically, I have seen far too many examples of unintended harm occur. I remember a typical example that occurred one summer when we were visiting some friends. My kids were in the back yard with their kids. Their six-year-old girl was playing fetch with the dog. The problem was that she was using a four-foot-long stick to do it. This created a danger for the other kids because, due to her immature coordination, she could have easily poked one of their eyes inadvertently when swinging or throwing the stick. Her father noticed the problem while observing the kids through the sliding glass door. Rightfully, he raced out to take care of the situation. Unfortunately, as he ran up behind his daughter to grab the stick, she cocked it just as he was approaching and accidentally caught him in the face. This enraged him. He grabbed the end of the stick and started spanking his girl with it. You can guess what happened next. It doesn't take a rocket scientist to figure out that the laws of physics were conspiring against this little girl. When you have a big strong man striking a small, weak child and you multiply the force with the adrenaline pumping from his anger times the length of the stick, you get a severely injured little girl. Naturally, her father was devastated that he had done what he did to his little girl. He never meant to hurt her and couldn't understand how it happened. Otherwise, he was a very good father.

Another similar incident happened with our neighbor in a supermarket. She had a two-year-old boy. As is typical with two-year-olds, he was running up and down the supermarket aisles creating a ruckus. His mother screamed at him to stop.

He didn't. So she raced up behind him, grabbed his arm, and jerked him back to get his attention. Unfortunately, the laws of physics were conspiring against this little two-year-old boy in much the same way as the previous incident. His mother had jerked his arm at a bad angle and pulled it right out of the shoulder socket. Again, the parent was horrified at what she had done. She couldn't understand how it happened. With the exception of this type of unfortunate accident, resulting from the use of physical punishment, she was otherwise a good mother.

I believe that at some level parents know it is not a good idea to deliberately hurt their children. Unfortunately, because they have so often been told that they must do so in order to be good parents, they force themselves to do so and then must rationalize their actions. I recently heard a father defend his spanking with this oft-stated rationalization, "It hurts me more than it hurts them." To that I say, "Bull. Your kids are the only ones getting hurt. You're hitting them. They haven't touched you."

The law of averages conspires against parents who use physical punishment. It lies in wait, ever patient, ready to lunge out and take its inevitable turn. This mathematical law tells us that every parent will end up injuring his child if he uses physical punishment long enough. Accidents are inevitable. It is impossible in the real world to avoid accidents. No one has ever had a perfect, accident-free record for any activity. If they have, it is only temporary. If they keep at it, an accident is guaranteed. Witness the space shuttle Challenger explosion, Chernobyl nuclear power plant meltdown, and Bophal chemical spill, to name a few well-known sensational accidents. More mundane accidents are fender benders or slipping on steps. I play racquetball for exercise. My partner and I are both mature adults who would never intentionally hit the other with the racquet. Guess how many times in the last ten years I've been clobbered with a racquet and injured? Even if I'm only accidently hit one out of 1,000 swings, the law of averages guarantees I will be hit with the racquet many times over the years. The same is true of disciplinary spanking, paddling or hitting. To err is human. Something will go wrong somewhere. The child will move, the adult will slip, or something, and an injury will occur, guaranteed. Since any act that results in the injury of a child is considered abuse by the majority (Sapp & Carter, 1978), and if the law of averages means that the routine use of physical punishment will eventually result in an injury, then corporal punishment must also be considered child abuse. The following article by Melissa Dribben (1999) indicates how often injury occurs.

The gurney flew over the false cheer of the purple threshold and into the trauma room in Children's Hospital. Doctors and nurses swarmed around the limp, bruised body of a 4-year-old boy. They grabbed for the tubes spilling out of one wall like plastic spaghetti. Beneath huge, white UFO lights, they worked desperately. At 7:15 a.m., the frenzy ceased. The room fell silent. Michael Davis had died from an apparent overdose of discipline. Discipline. This is what Jane McBurrows is calling the way her husband sometimes smacked the children in his care, or used a belt instead of a tongue-lashing to keep them in line. In her statement to investigators, she said her husband, the Rev. Javan M. McBurrows, spanked Michael for wetting his pants and sneaking a peek at two girls in the family bathtub. You know there has to be more to this story. It will all come out in court. Mr. McBurrows is expected to be charged with murdering the boy, whose mother placed him and two of his sisters in the pastor's care. But this is a crime whose dismal echo will be heard long after the killer has gone to jail. For whoever walloped that child beyond an inch of his life was not very original. Bones don't break easily, Dr. Joanne Decker sees beaten babies all the time. "There are different levels of abuse," said Decker, who was in the ER at Children's Hospital yesterday. "I see children who've been hurt from overzealous discipline maybe every other shift. The devastating injuries, about once a month." Decker, who has two small children of her own, says she understands how exasperating they can be. She sympathizes with parents who run out of patience. She recently treated an 11-month-old girl whose grandmother had broken the baby's arm, trying to put on her undershirt. "It's not easy to break a child's bones," said Decker. "But when someone's forthright about what happened, and clearly upset like this woman was, you can help." What doesn't help is the widespread belief that it's really OK to hit a kid—and that it's the severity, not the principle, that's a problem. "Most Americans believe in corporal punishment, and there are studies that show that 95 percent spank their children," said Dr. Cindy Christian of Children's Hospital, a specialist in shaken-baby syndrome. In most cases, the whupping parents dispense in the name of love does not approach deadly force. But it can. What lesson is learned? "In many cases of child abuse, there is no intent to kill," said Christian. "The problem is uncontrolled violence and aggression. It's a lack of self-control on the part of the adult. They're striking out in anger and frustration." And whether that frustration leads to a welt on the backside or to a broken bone, it's not healthy. It may be efficient to hit a disobedient kid to get him to stop what he's doing. But you can't call it a lesson in how to behave. "Corporal punishment is a punishment, not a discipline," said Christian. It is her opinion that smacking a child is a hypocritical way to teach nonviolence or self-control. It gets the point across that you're upset, but implies that it's all right for a big person to hurt a small one. It's her professional experience that when a 150-pound adult uses physical force on a 20-pound child, the result can be tragic, if not deadly. The McBurrowses, who lived in squalor, chronic debt and conflict, are not typical in any way. But they occupy a place on the dangerous line that connects a smack across the cheeks to a fractured skull. No 4-year-old deserves to be hit for having trouble controlling his bladder. No boy that young and innocent should be hurt and made to feel there's something wrong or dirty about seeing the children in his own family naked. This story did not begin or end with Mr. McBurrows. The beating goes on as we stand complicit—in silence and ignorance, if not in action.

Reprinted with permission from The Philadelphia Inquirer.

There is another insidious psychological effect in operation when parents use corporal punishment on their children that results in hostile feelings toward their children and the increased likelihood of causing them physical harm. It is called *cognitive dissonance* or *self justification* (Ch. 3). It can occur if parents spank their children when they are angry at them. Psychological research shows that there is a tendency to engage in overkill when punishing under these conditions. Kahn (1966) performed several experiments to find out what would happen when one retaliates against someone who did something disturbing or hurtful. He had someone pose as a medical technician who took physiological measurements and made derogatory remarks about students who signed up to participate in an experiment. Half the students were allowed to express their hostile feelings by complaining to the technician's employer, who responded by threatening to get the technician into serious trouble, possibly even fire him. The other half of the students in the experiment were not allowed to express any aggression toward the technician who had made them angry. Which group do you think ended up with the most residual feelings of hostility toward the technician? Most people would answer that it was the group that was not allowed to vent their anger. But that's not what happened. Those in the group who expressed their aggression later felt greater dislike and hostility toward the technician. In other words, expressing aggression, as in spanking a child, increases feelings of hostility toward the target and increases the desire and probability for further aggression in the future. This can become the impetus for a vicious cycle of increasing hostility and aggression toward a child for parents who use corporal punishment to discipline. The self-justification effect explains why this happens. When you harm someone, it sets into motion a cognitive process that attempts to justify why you harmed that person, especially if the victim has not done anything harmful to you. Cognitive dissonance will occur. This means you have two incompatible thoughts and will be highly motivated to reduce the dissonance by rationalizing. Here is what typically happens: The thought (cognition), "I have hurt Johnny," is incompatible (dissonant) with the thought, "I am a decent, caring parent." You can reduce the dissonance by convincing yourself that hurting Johnny was a reasonable thing to do. You can accomplish this by diminishing Johnny's virtues and emphasizing his faults. In other words, "I behaved reasonably by hurting Johnny because he is a bad kid who deserved to be hurt." This sets the stage for further physical aggression against Johnny in the future, especially since committing a violent act the first time reduces one's inhibitions and makes it easier to do a second time.

If this sounds artificial, it shouldn't. Just look at the world around us. These exact dynamics occur all the time. Take sporting events, for example. Soccer games require tight security in Europe due to the behavior of what are known as "soccer hooligans." When they aggress against innocent opposing fans by calling them names, they eventually come to justify their actions by denigrating them to the extent that they eventually feel that they deserve to be attacked physically and end up in a melee. The prevalence of gang warfare can be explained in the same manner, as can genocide. So can the beatings that occur in riots and hate crimes. It also explains why the victorious members of a nation who have just won a war seldom feel much sympathy for the innocent victims of wartime bombings.

We justify these actions of aggression by adopting increasingly derogatory attitudes toward the enemy. This justifies our own destructiveness. Most Americans do not feel much sympathy for the innocent civilian victims of our wars against the citizens of Germany (Dresden fire-storm), Japan (Tokyo fire-storm), Vietnam (bombing of Hanoi), or Iraq (bombing of Bagdad). The psychological dynamic of denigrating those that we aggress against in order to justify our actions is what underlies the shocking statistics on child abuse, which of course often begins as "mere" physical punishment, as is apparent in the following tragic case of little Tedi McGeary.

MAN GETS 4 1/2–20 YEARS IN JAIL
FOR CHILD-SHAKING INJURIES
BY JAN ACKERMAN (1995), POST-GAZETTE STAFF WRITER—
In the stillness of a nearly filled courtroom, the hum of the air conditioner and the sound of lawyers shuffling papers were punctuated by Tedi McGeary's guttural sounds, which only her mother seemed to understand. Tedi turned four yesterday, but she cannot speak or walk, is paralyzed on the right side and will need constant care the rest of her life.

Yesterday, Douglas Bishop, the man who was convicted of shaking her so hard that part of her brain had to be removed, apologized to the child's mother, Sarah McGeary of Moon, while the child's muffled sounds could be heard in the background. "I never intended to injure anyone," said Bishop, 33, of Richland who, during his trial, had denied doing anything to harm the child. "A little too late," McGeary said outside court, adding that Bishop made the apology only because "his own life was on the line." The child was injured on Aug. 28, 1993, while Bishop was baby-sitting in his home. Common Pleas Judge Jeffrey A. Manning, who characterized the shaking as "stupid but unintentional," sentenced Bishop to 4 1/2 to 20 years in prison. A jury on June 8 convicted Bishop of aggravated assault, reckless endangerment, and endangering the welfare of children. "I am convinced that you lost your temper and shook this child," Manning told Bishop. "I am convinced that you didn't even know what you were doing."

McGreary said she was satisfied with the sentence. Manning denied defense attorney Kim Riester's request for bond pending appeal and ordered Bishop to pay McGeary $1,500 a month in restitution for every month he is on parole.

Rester said that Bishop's home insurance company, which covered negligent acts that occurred on the premises, might have paid part of McGeary's medical bills if Bishop had been allowed to plead guilty to lesser charges. Once Bishop was convicted of aggravated assault, Riester said, the homeowners policy would not pay.

Tedi's bills are astronomical, her mother said, adding that the bill for two weeks of care in a hospital's ICU unit was $198,000. She said her life has become filled with wheelchairs, braces, rehabilitation equipment, and constant attention to Tedi's needs.

At yesterday's sentencing, Tedi was in constant motion, grabbing her mother's arm, sucking her own thumb, stuffing toys in her mouth and occasionally crying "Mama" or "Oh-Oh," the only words she can articulate. "She cannot do anything for herself as hard as she tries," McGeary said. "She can never be left alone and must always be in the supervised care of at least one adult." Tedi's eyesight and hearing were impaired and she has a plastic plate in her head that will have to be replaced as she grows. McGeary, 26, said she quit her job and went on welfare so that she could care for Tedi.

"Despite all of our hardships, Tedi is perfect and we will make it. We are not looking for pity; all we want is justice," McGeary said.

Chapter 5

Creating Well-Behaved Children
Without Spanking

If the research findings in the preceding three chapters are correct, in that they show that spanking creates more problems than it solves, then we would not expect spanking to work very well for typical parents in controlling their child's behavior. This is exactly what we find is the case in households where spanking is used as the main form of behavior control. This point is demonstrated in the case of Sheri Cooper Sinykin (1983), who articulated exceptionally well in a REDBOOK article how the use of spanking was a dismal failure for her:

> I have always loved my son Aaron, but I have to admit there was a time when I didn't much like him. His increasing aggressiveness toward others—in particular toward his baby brother, Rudi—frightened and angered me. Once I found him desperately trying to take a toy away from Rudi, and the toy's cord was wrapped around Rudi's neck. Even though I realized that at the age of three Aaron was too young to foresee the consequences of his action, I feared for Rudi's safety. After more than two years of being an only child, Aaron was used to getting what he wanted, especially my attention. Naturally I assumed that jealousy was the reason for his hostile behavior. I found out later that I was wrong.
>
> My husband, Daniel, thought I was exaggerating when I recounted my daily trials. "Everything will be all right,"

he'd say. "He's probably going through a phase." Unfortunately, Daniel's work as an attorney and land developer kept him busy most weekends and several evenings a week. He rarely saw Aaron's animosity. To him, Aaron remained a pleasant, good-humored child who gave him affection for the price of a piece of gum at the end of a long, hard day.

I researched the problem by reading "all" the parenting books and tried out the advice of well-meaning friends and relatives. Nothing worked. Aaron was like a sponge, absorbing from me every drop of attention he could get by continually assaulting eleven-month old Rudi, his toys and the children of our friends. His uncanny ability to send even bigger boys running to their mothers in tears frustrated me. How could a twenty-eight-pound child wield so much power, especially over me? In quiet moments of honesty I admitted my anger at myself for not knowing how to control him. *I am his mother*, I kept thinking. *I should know what to do.* But I didn't. Finally I told Daniel I'd be willing to forgo the Caribbean cruise we'd talked about taking if it meant that Aaron—and I—would get help. Only then did he realize just how concerned I was about finding a solution to our problem. Our children's pediatrician, Dr. Curtis Weatherhogg, recommended the state's Home and Community Treatment Program at the Mendota Mental Health Institute, here in Madison, Wisconsin. Dr. Weatherhogg told us that program staff members would come into our home and observe how we all got along together. Then Daniel and I would be trained in communicating and disciplinary skills designed to make Aaron toe the line. After the training period, staffers would come into our home again to help us use our new skills successfully.

The program seemed perfect from my standpoint, but

after our first meeting the staffers told us that Aaron wasn't considered "disturbed enough" to qualify under the current state guidelines. Sensing our frustration and our eagerness for their help, they and our pediatrician persevered to find a loophole. A few weeks later Dr. Weatherhogg told us that the staffers had agreed to teach Gayle, one of the nurses in his office, their techniques and use us as guinea pigs.

We told Aaron that three women, Molly, Mary Ann and Gayle, would be spending a lot of time at our house to see how we all got along. "Will they help you be happy at me?" he asked.

I told him I hoped so. But even as we tried to prepare Aaron for the home observation I felt anxious and ill-prepared. How could I act as I usually did—losing my temper or repeating myself umpteen times—in front of three strangers? Whatever confidence I'd had in my mothering abilities dwindled as our first observation date approached. But I knew if I really wanted help, I would have to behave as natural as possible.

Molly, Mary Ann and Gayle visited us four times that month, observing us literally morning, noon and night. They saw us at our best and at our worst. No matter what went on around them, they never said a word until the session's end. What they shared then was neither threatening nor judgmental, and I lapped up all their "good" comments with genuine thirst. I finally began feeling that I was an okay mother, with the promise of becoming an even better one.

After their fourth visit, the team called Daniel, the children and me together at Dr. Weatherhogg's office to give us their impression of what we were doing well already and what they felt they could help us with. They said that Daniel and I had problems giving Aaron clear messages and directions. They pointed out that, for example, when he was kicking his trucks across the room one of us would say, "Aaron? What are you doing? Why are you kicking your toys," instead of, "Aaron! Stop! Toys are not for kicking!"

The team said they sensed that we didn't really know what to do when Aaron was naughty. They were right. Spanking seemed more a way to express our frustrations than a way to teach Aaron to behave, and I always apologized guiltily afterward anyway, diluting whatever impact the spanking might have made. Sending Aaron to his room didn't help—he was likely to peel off the wallpaper. Another problem was that Aaron's precocious vocabulary had seduced us into believing that he understood more than he actually did. Consequently our expectations were too high.

The team's over all impression was that Aaron controlled our behavior instead of our controlling his. His aggression wasn't the problem; it was merely one of the tactics he used to get our attention. Neither was Aaron particularly jealous of Rudi; the team said his assaults were calculated more to bring us running than to hurt his brother. They had also observed that Aaron was skillful at tuning us out or distracting us—"Watch what he does. Don't listen to what he says," they advised. And see how he's getting out of obeying any and every request.

Leaving Aaron at nursery school and Rudi with a friend, Daniel and I met with the team three more times at the pediatrician's office to learn how to deal with Aaron's behavior. In the first session we discussed how to "set the stage" so that Aaron was likelier to behave well. We needed to agree upon a set of "house rules," which both Daniel and I were to enforce. We were taught to "play act" new situations with Aaron and to talk with him ahead of time about how he would behave at bedtime and even at such special events as a birthday party. Part of our problem was that we assumed Aaron knew how to behave, when in fact he hadn't the slightest idea about what was expected of him.

The second session focused on Aaron's behavior. We learned that saying "Stop doing this or that" does not teach the child what good behavior you expect him to perform instead. Saying "Stop! Put your hands in your pockets" is more effective than "Stop touching things." We learned that everything a child does is designed to win him attention, and for Aaron, it didn't really matter if attention came in the form of hugs or spankings. We learned how important it was for us to place a higher value on our attention, awarding it only when Aaron did something "good" and withdrawing it when he acted up.

The hardest thing was learning to give clear directions and remembering not to repeat them. I had a terrible habit of saying things like, "Aaron, please pick up your toys, okay?" He'd say "Huh?" at least once, I'd repeat myself, and then he'd think, *No, it's not okay. I don't want to pick them up.* It took a lot of practice for me to be able to think out exactly what I wanted him to do, get his attention by calling his name or touching his arm and then saying only once "Aaron, I want you please to pick up your toys right now."

The final session dealt with "consequences," and it pulled together everything we'd learned. The consequence of good behavior is praise, praise, praise, as well as hugs, kisses, and any special treats you may want to bestow. At first it felt awkward to praise Aaron for "sitting still" or "looking at me" when I spoke or "walking carefully by Rudi." When he wasn't bothering me, it was much easier to get busy with something and ignore him rather than to remember to praise him for whatever good thing he was doing. The benefits of praise, however, became clear almost overnight.

But learning what to do when Aaron misbehaved and doing it successfully proved to be two different things. I was so grateful for the final phase of the program, when Molly, Mary Ann, and Gayle came back to our house several times over the next three months, actually stepping in and showing me exactly what to do. Whenever Aaron hurt people or property, I was taught to give him a "time-out" from whatever he was doing, removing him to a quiet corner away from people, toys, and television. I learned to be calm but stern in making sure that he sat cross-legged on the floor for thirty seconds to two minutes, depending on the circumstances. Then I'd say something like "Aaron, your time-out is over. Please come here and let's think of a way you can get Rudi to give you your toy back without hitting him." We'd talk together, and Aaron might say, "I can give him his toy or I can call you for help." Then I'd look on as Aaron tried out his ideas, and the time-out sequence always ended with my praising Aaron for doing "something nice" such as kissing, hugging, or getting a toy for his brother.

The changes in Aaron came more quickly than we'd ever expected. He even began responding to my requests that he do things he disliked, such as collecting the trash. He discovered new ways to "be nice to Rudi" and delighted in showing me. And buoyed by intermittent praise, he started playing by himself for increasingly longer periods of time.

We kept marveling at Aaron's growth, but our own growth was just as astonishing. I gradually realized that anger and frustration were no longer daily emotions. I knew exactly how to handle whatever mischief Aaron might throw my way—without nagging, yelling or spanking. When we emerged from our four and a half months in the program, our reactions to Aaron's behavior were not perfect but they were much better than they had been. The other day Rudi was blocking Aaron's view of the television and Aaron shoved him away. In the "old days" I would have yelled at him, perhaps even spanked him if I was at my wits' end. That day I calmly said, "Aaron, time-out," and he immediately and sheepishly served time in the corner. Afterward he showed me how he could gently lead Rudi away from the television screen, distracting him with a toy. That is progress.

It hasn't been easy to change my relationship with Aaron. I take it one day at a time, realizing that both of us can have "off" days occasionally. Now when things go "badly," they're still better than I had ever dreamed possible. The other day Aaron actually gave Rudi a lollipop he'd received as a treat at school; a few days before, he spontaneously offered his brother a favor and a balloon he'd brought home from a birthday party. In time it may be easy to forget the way things used to be, but I hope I never do. That memory keeps me grateful for the miracle of daily laughter in our lives, especially Aaron's and Rudi's—and mine.

Reprinted with permission from Sheri Cooper Sinykin.

This story exemplifies practically everything that can go wrong when spanking is used. Here is a mother who realized spanking was more the problem than the cure and fortunately found alternative methods of discipline that worked much better. How did Aaron turn out you may be wondering? Ms. Sinykin recently provided me with an update. Although Aaron, now 24, was bothered by the "spoiled brat" REDBOOK headline as he was growing up, he has "turned out fine," she reported. "He is now married and happily employed as a financial analyst at INTEL. Aaron and Rudi are now friends. I hope stories like mine give parents hope that the tensions of childhood can, indeed, be resolved with good parenting skills."

The spanking alternatives that Sheri Cooper Sinykin used so successfully will be the subject matter of this chapter. But keep in mind, as you try out these alternatives, that nothing works perfectly 100% of the time with toddlers, and kids in general. They are human and humans are not perfect, especially kid humans. Give these discipline techniques a fair chance. Don't discard them and go back to spanking based upon one, a few failures, or a lot of failures. In fact, we know that no matter what type of discipline parents use when telling a child not to do something again, there is a ninety-plus percent chance he will do it again. With kids, there will always be many failures. They have less maturity, reasoning ability, and control than adults, shorter attention spans, and they are more forgetful and impulsive. They are immature because their brains are not fully developed and will not be until about the age of eighteen. Keep this reality in mind and make allowances for it. Expecting perfection is asking way too much. If you do, you will be doomed to untold frustration and failure. The point is, that over the long haul, these suggested techniques will lead to better outcomes, not perfection.

There are many advantages to using non-physical forms of discipline. One of the main advantages is that it creates a warm and positive family climate versus a fearful, cold and threatening one. Family members are more likely to feel good about each other when family interactions focus on positive rather than negative behaviors. Children who get recognition for what they do right have higher self-esteem than those who are attacked for wrongdoing.

It is unfortunate that we use the word "discipline" when we are referring to teaching our kids how to behave. Words carry powerful connotations. They can have a powerful impact on our attitudes and behaviors. For instance, the word "mental illness" carries a heavy stigma to the point that many people who suffer from it will not seek help. The reason is that it carries the connotation of weakness, poor character, embarrassment, failure, and being an outcast. If we changed the terminology of mental health and used such words as "facilitator" and "quality of life" to portray the treatment of mental illness, people would be much more eager to take advantage of it. Doesn't it sound much more enticing to say "I have to go see my facilitator today to improve my quality of life," as opposed to "I have to go see my psychotherapist for my mental illness?" Likewise, parents would do better to think in terms of providing their children with direction rather than discipline. The word "direction" creates a mind-set that makes it more acceptable to use nonviolent parenting techniques when raising children. Discipline connotes negative images of spanking, harshness, intimidation, commanding, blind obedience, destructiveness, and punishment. In contrast, providing children with direction connotes images of teaching, positive role modeling, guidance, nurturing, rewarding, and being constructive and respectful.

Baumrind (1971, 1978) found that the optimal parenting pattern, authoritative parenting, consists of firmly setting controls and limits, but in a warm fashion, emphasizing affection, nurturance, and acceptance. In contrast, authoritarian parents emphasize discipline and are low on warmth. Their children were not as well-adjusted. Poor child management techniques are related to children's use of alcohol, cigarettes, illicit drugs, and other acting-out and control problems (Dishion, Patterson, & Reid, 1988). Drug use in children is predicted by parental lack of affection, detachment, lack of acceptance, weak or excessive control, and inconsistency (Kandel, 1990). Positive parenting techniques produce well-adjusted children because they combine the parental control of limit-setting and guidance with warmth and nurturance. An emphasis on affection, nurturance, involvement, and acceptance, rather than punitive discipline, produces the optimal outcome (Kandel, 1990; Maccoby & Martin, 1983).

Why Some Parents Have Decided to Quit Hitting

Davis (1999) interviewed twenty-two parents who made a concerted effort to stop using corporal punishment on their children in order to uncover common reasons behind the decision to quit hitting, slapping, and spanking. One twenty-eight-year-old mother felt guilty over her daughter's cowering and fear:

> One time when she was about four years old, I had spanked her maybe a week before, and she had done something that made me really angry and I wanted to spank her and she just cowered away, and it made me feel like I was an abusive parent. She was afraid of me at that point and that made me feel terrible 'cause she was a little two-foot baby, four years old, and I'm . . . a big lady to her. So it just made me feel bad that she was really afraid.

A thirty-seven-year-old mother of two girls said she was moved to quit after seeing her daughter spank a doll. She did not like the fact that she had modeled the practice of hitting. "That was the most important thing in all of this, when I saw her smacking that doll. She couldn't have been more than sixteen or eighteen months. I went to him and told my husband we are not going to do this." Another mother, twenty-seven years old, raising a five year old daughter and fifteen-month-old boy realized spanking was ineffective, that it did not do any good. She observed that it just made her children angrier and less cooperative. "It got to the point where if I gave her a spanking she would just lay in her room and just scream at me. She was so mad that I had spanked her, and I found that it just didn't do any good at all, it just made the situation worse. At this point, I just don't believe in spanking . . . I've come to realize it just doesn't do any good." An African American mother, after she became a counselor at a battered women's shelter, observed a connection between spanking, domestic violence, and battered women. "My past child rearing did include spanking because that is how I was reared. But I became a counselor for abused women and their children, and that's when I learned alternative methods to spanking. I've pretty much implemented those things . . . and it's worked." Another African American mother changed her mind after joining the Baha'i faith. "Baha'i's are told that—using the analogy that Arabian horses aren't hit because it ruins the horse—children are much more important than horses so we shouldn't hit our children. That's what stuck in my mind as the reason for not hitting children." There is a common theme among these parents' decision to quit hitting their children: They searched inward and rethought old ideas. They reached a turning point in which they saw spanking in a new light about right and wrong, violence and nonviolence, respect, and childrens' rights.

Why it is so hard to convince parents to give up spanking?

Recently an irate school vice principal called me on the phone after he had read a newspaper article in which I was quoted as saying that spanking doesn't work. He said I was dead wrong because corporal punishment has worked fine for him for the last twenty years both in the school with students and at home with his children. He was absolutely certain that I was wrong because his personal experience contradicted what I said. In his experience he found that he had to use corporal punishment at school, and spanking at home, for misbehavior because it worked, while praising good behavior had not worked for him. Why did he maintain this mistaken belief? There is an interesting finding in experimental psychology that may provide the answer.

Regression toward the mean

Many parents likewise will abandon a newly-tried discipline technique, quickly decide that it does not work, return to spanking, and conclude that spanking works much better. What causes them to believe this when, in reality, spanking is inferior and gets poorer results? The answer lies in the fact that they are succumbing to a statistical phenomenon called *regression toward the mean* (McBurney, 1996). This was discovered by an early psychologist, Sir Francis Galton, in the nineteenth century in his studies of hereditary traits. He noticed that tall men tend to have shorter sons and short men generally have taller sons. Those men who fall in the extremes of height will generally have sons whose height is closer to the mean, or average, height. It occurs often in behavior, too. A parent of either extremely high or low intelligence will tend to have children whose IQ is closer to the average than their parent. The reason this happens is that for extremes of behavior to occur, a rare combination of events must conspire to make it occur. This could be called luck. Good luck, by definition, does not occur every time. It rarely occurs twice in a row. Someone may win the million dollar lottery today, but what are the odds that she'll win the same million dollar lottery tomorrow? It is practically nonexistent. She'll probably have to wait a good many years to win again, if ever. The same thing occurs in nature and extremes of human behavior. An example of this is the *Sports Illustrated* jinx. The performance of athletes who appear on the cover of *Sports Illustrated* appears to nose dive right after they appear. This is due to the regression toward the mean effect rather than the widely believed *Sports Illustrated* jinx. Athletes who have recently performed great feats are chosen to appear. This means that that rare combination of health, circumstance, and luck have conspired to create a moment or period of great achievement. Everything coming together perfectly in one's life is unsustainable. Hence, the inevitable fall.

This phenomenon creates a problem in interpreting the effects of a behavioral intervention. For instance, let's take an example of a father whose kids are acting up. He shows great restraint all day until finally their ruckus reaches a crescendo. It's more than he can take so he snaps, gives them all a sound spanking, and yells that they'd better knock it off or they'll get more of the same. The father notices that immediately after the spanking the kids are better behaved and concludes that the spanking worked. The problem is that, even though his observation is correct, his conclusion that spanking works is wrong. Due to regression toward the mean, it was inevitable that the kids behavior would improve after they behaved particularly bad, *even if no spanking had occurred.* To make matters even worse, the father may have tried to follow the advice of behavioral scientists by rewarding his children when they displayed particularly good behavior. Lo and behold, he noticed that afterwards their behavior deteriorated, so he extends his conclusion to include the fact that praise is useless, in addition to his previous observation that the way to teach children how to behave is by spanking them.

Had the school vice principal, who concluded that spanking works much better than praise, been open to alternative explanations for his personal observations, I would have explained how the phenomenon of regression toward the mean works. But he, like many parents, is more interested in hearing explanations that justify his preconceptions than those that contradict them.

Negative Reinforcement

Another thing that parents have to realize in making the switch from spanking to other forms of discipline is why most parents use spanking. First, it is much easier to spank than to figure out how to reinforce more desirable behaviors and other creative forms of behavior control. Also, when we are angry it is naturally reinforcing to punish someone because the relief of venting that anger is satisfying to us. Unfortunately, this, in time, turns spanking into something that is really more for the benefit of the punisher than the punished. The benefit for parents is the tension-relieving properties of spanking, hence its reinforcing (negative) function. The punisher is compelled to continue punishing due to negative reinforcement. Behavior that brings about the elimination of something unpleasant is negatively reinforced. Spanking behavior is negatively reinforced in two ways: It eliminates pent-up frustration through venting and it temporarily stops the irritating behavior that is being punished. A mother who is extremely frustrated and annoyed by her children's behavior, and spanks them as a result, will feel the relief provided by the negative reinforcement of her spanking, first when spanking the kids vents her frustration, and secondly when her annoyance at the kids' behavior diminishes once they cease doing what they got punished for.

Social Traps

Spanking is a type of social trap. Social trap behavior is difficult to change. Garrett Hardin (1968) described this phenomenon in his classic article entitled "The Tragedy of the Commons." He noticed that the cow pastures on private land were in better shape than the public, or common, pasture lands. He reasoned that when people are free to pursue their own interests, they will do so at the expense of the public good. This is why common pasture lands all over the world are overgrazed. If each farmer would limit the size of his herd, there would be enough grazing land for everyone. But unfortunately, people are more inclined to act in their own personal, concrete best interest than the amorphous, abstract publics' best interest. By contrast, a farmer who overgrazed his own land would only be hurting himself, not the abstract "public," so consequently he is much more inclined to take better care of it. With common lands, each individual farmer thinks, "I need to finance a new barn," or "I need a larger tractor," and decides to add to the size of his herd. Each reasons that they are only creating a small increase in the size of the herd relative to the size of the commons. All 100 farmers will be thinking "I'm only adding five cattle, the common pasture can support that many more." However, that kind of individual thinking times 100 farmers actually adds 500 cattle to the commons. Eventually, the land is overgrazed and depleted to the point where it cannot sustain anyone's herd. These social traps are occurring all over the world and creating enormous problems. Examples are the depletion of fisheries and forests, acid rain, polluted water, traffic jams, and overpopulation. People yield to immediate rewards while ignoring long-term costs. That is why people are inclined to drink too much now even though they will pay the cost later with a hangover, or they succumb to getting a deep, dark tan to look good now to the opposite sex, even though they will pay a heavy toll later in life with over-aged, damaged skin and possibly even skin cancer. Spanking is another type of social trap. For most, when using spanking, the immediate benefits of venting anger and eliminating the annoying behavior, are too rewarding to consider the long-term costs of the thirteen undesirable adverse side effects of spanking.

Parents' Personal Problems

The heavy reliance on physical punishment in some families is often a symptom of other problems. Parents can be under tremendous stress, due to problems like unemployment, marital discord, low frustration tolerance, lack of coping mechanisms, financial strain, a heavy work load, or other

responsibilities. Unfortunately, this stress is sometimes manifested in hitting the kids. Dysfunctional families may use a
certain child as a scapegoat for the family and "punish" him
accordingly. This can serve the purpose of providing a handy
explanation for what is wrong in the family, thus allowing
everyone else in the family off the hook by not having to
examine their own role in the family's dysfunction. Sometimes
maladjusted parents may bully their children physically to
inappropriately meet their power and control needs. This signi-
fies emotional immaturity in the parents. Parental mental
illness, drug addiction, or antisocial personality disorder may
also lead to abusive discipline practices. Children with certain
medical conditions can tax even the most saintly of parents.
Children with disabilities are more likely to be abused (Westat,
1993). Many parents of children with such problems as
Attention Deficit-Hyperactivity Disorder, Tourettes Syndrome,
Fetal Alcohol Syndrome, allergies, or chronic pain, for
instance, find it difficult to not lash out in frustration at their
children, at times, especially if the child's disorder is not diag-
nosed, and the parents believe they or the child are at fault for
the behavior problems (Day, Peterson, McCracken, 1998).
Many of the above problems that may compel parents to resort
to physical punishment may require professional treatment
before the problem of disciplining style can be effectively
addressed. Oftentimes, distressed, and otherwise normal
parents overestimate the capabilities of their children and
expect too much from them.

The Homunculus Myth

Parent's misconceptions about childhood development and
their attitudes toward children in general can have a directive
influence on their disciplinary practices. For instance, if a
parent believed in the *Homunculus Myth of Development*, that
children are merely little adults, with all the same abilities, but
just in a smaller package, they may demand too much of them

and punish them for failing to live up to the parents' unreasonable demands. Parents who are heavy users of physical punishment often are ignorant about normal child development and consequently have unrealistically high expectations of their children's behavior (Steel & Pollack, 1968). I have seen this problem occur quite frequently. Piaget (1967), the late eminent developmental psychologist, in his studies of cognitive development, found that children under the age of seven are egocentric. They believe everyone else experiences the world exactly as they do. That is why a four-year-old girl will typically want to buy a doll, if pressed by her father to chose a Christmas present for her mother. She believes everyone wants the same thing she wants. A four-year-old boy might hold up a new toy to the telephone and say, "See what I got for my birthday, Grandma!" He believes everyone else sees exactly what he is looking at.

That's why preschoolers find it so difficult to share their toys with playmates. They think that if "I want this toy" then everyone wants me to have this toy, too. They cannot put themselves in another person's place and see the world from that perspective. Piaget tested this by showing young children a two-sided mirror (Piaget, 1952). He then looked in one side and had the child look in the other side. The child, upon being asked, "Who do you see in the mirror?" would answer, "Me." When asked by the experimenter, "Who do I see in the mirror?" the child still responded with "Me." All too often I have seen parents scold and punish their preschoolers for not sharing. This results from not understanding the maturational sequence of cognitive abilities.

It is harder for parents to recognize psychological limitations than it is for physical ones. We readily provide children with no-spill cups and diapers because their physical development is incomplete. How can parents accurately gauge their children's cognitive limitations? A good indicator of how a child's cognitive and emotional development are progressing is their physical maturation. If the child has physical limitations, then she probably has an equal degree of cognitive limitations. They parallel each other. We can tell what's happening on the inside by looking at the outside. A typical parent would recognize the folly of trying to toilet train a six-month-old infant. Parents understand that the brain structures that control the bowel muscles are not developed. However, they rarely stop to question whether or not the cognitive brain structures are developed that allow a child to feel empathy for another. That is why too many parents end up ridiculing or putting down a preschooler for not sharing by saying such things as, "Why are you so selfish? Don't you care about anyone but yourself?" Any subsequent punishments are useless and just as ineffective as trying to toilet train a child before he has developed the brain structures that permit him to use the potty. The outcome will not be a change in sharing behavior, but more likely disappointment and frustration for the parent and lowered self-esteem in the child. We easily recognize physical limitations in children's development. We need to equally allow for children's cognitive limitations. Not only do mistaken attitudes about how much we should expect from children lead to a heavy-handed discipline style, but so does our attitude about what causes kids to act the way they do.

Attribution Bias

Parental attitudes play a major role in discipline practices. If one's philosophy or world view about children or their roles is that they are inherently bad; they are a nuisance that interferes with a parent's enjoyment of life; they are deliberately trying to annoy me; they are not as important as adults; they do not deserve respect; their purpose is to meet adults' needs, or one simply does not like kids, then harsh, punitive, and physical punishments will likely be the preferred method of discipline. Research in the area of social cognition indicates that parents' belief in the causes of their children's behavior is related to the type of discipline they choose to practice (Himelstein, Graham, & Weiner, 1991). The word *attribution,* as used in psychology, means "to what do we attribute the cause of people's behavior?" Social psychologists use the term *attributional bias* when people think about what causes others' behavior and misattribute the cause. An example of this would be the belief that those on welfare are lazy. The bias is the tendency to attribute people's failures (to get a job, in this case) to an internal flaw, such as laziness, rather than to circumstances, such as getting laid off work. For instance: *is my child behaving badly because I spared the rod and spoiled the child, or because he is a "bad seed" or willfully disobedient?* The former is a *situational attribution* (the cause of the child's bad behavior was a permissive situation) and the latter is a *dispositional* one (the cause resides inside the child's personality).

A typical bias in attributions is the parent's belief that the child is behaving badly on purpose just to torment him, "Why is he doing this to me?" The accurate attribution would be: "He's not doing this to me on purpose; he's just engaging in age-appropriate behavior." This and other negative attributional biases, such as the belief that a very young child should have known better but misbehaved anyway (a dispositional attribution) so he needs to be disciplined, are more pronounced in the parents of children who are abused and aggressive than among other parents (Compas, Adelman, Freundl, Nelson, & Taylor, 1982). It stands to reason that a parent who believes that her child's behavior results mainly from the type of discipline she deploys, is going to be much more amenable to change and willing to try new discipline practices, than a parent who believes that the source of a child's misconduct is in his inherent disposition, the so-called "willfully disobedient" child.

Regression toward the mean, negative reinforcement, social traps, personal problems, the Homunculus Myth, and attribution bias are not the only explanation for parents' excessive reliance on physical punishment. There is also human nature at play. Switching forms of discipline implies that what one has been doing all these years is wrong, and people generally hate to admit that they are wrong. It is much easier to avoid the guilt of knowing what one did to his children was seriously wrong by steadfastly maintaining one's belief in the effectiveness of corporal punishment. It is so much harder for parents to face the reality that they are unnecessarily exposing their children to the risk of serious harm.

Political and religious ideology also influence parental discipline attitudes. Eisenman and Sirgo (1991) examined the parenting attitudes of twenty-five liberals and twenty-five conservatives. They measured parents' preferences about two opposing styles of parenting, allowing children to learn on their own (internal) versus a preference for parental dominance and control (external). Of those who were classified as liberals, 88% preferred internal child rearing while 76% of the conservatives expressed the opposite preference—they preferred to use external, parentally-controlled child rearing. This translated into more external and punitive control of their children. Conservatives emphasized parental control through the use of physical punishment, preferring an orderly, unchanging type of life. Liberals, on the other hand, were more tolerant of their children's behavior and unlikely to favor physical punishment. Ironically, the authors pointed out that by using physical punishment, conservatives may end up with the type of children they do not want. Kandel (1990) found that the children of parents who use physical, punitive discipline have difficulty controlling their behavior, are aggressive, and disobedient. He speculates that excessive control through the use of external punishment by parents does not allow children to think independently nor learn to use internal control mechanisms, so they have difficulty learning self-control. An example of how this political philosophy plays out legislatively occurred in California. In 1994 an American youth was sentenced to be caned (beaten with a stick) for vandalism he committed while in Singapore. Three California assemblymen pushed a proposal to adopt a similar practice in the United States. The Republican Assemblyman from Orange County, California, was quoted as saying, "My goal is to humble these punks early on so we don't see them later in court as murderers." (*Wheeling Intelligencer*, May 27, 1994). This reminds me of the thinking from a past civilization. The Maya believed they could stop catastrophes by sacrificing human beings. The tragedy is that, in their ignorance, the only catastrophe that ever occurred was caused by their "preventive" actions.

Finally, cultural norms that condone corporal punishment are at work. They not only permit spanking, but virtually demand it. Since the vast majority of parents spank, then those who do not become the deviants in our society (the word *deviant* is meant in the sociological sense, *those in the minority*. It is more popularly termed "different"). Sociologists tell us, and most people already know, that the majority will exert a great deal of pressure to conform on those who are different. Carson (1986) found that parents who chose not to spank their children were criticized for their choice by friends and family members and pressured to use corporal punishment.

Most parents will be reluctant to switch discipline techniques for these reasons and others. But, if you can resist the temptation to stay with the status quo, the psychological research virtually guarantees that you will be highly rewarded for your efforts to change. Those rewards include a closer bond between parent and child, a child who feels better about herself, a child who is guided by her own conscience and not dependent on force to do what is right, and a less aggressive child. I have evidence from the testimonials of former students that I have run into that this is not just theoretical, that it actually happens in the real world. They have told me that they were very pleased with the outcome of the alternative discipline methods. They said that they never felt very good about spanking anyway, but just did not know of any alternatives until they learned about them as a student in my psychology classes. I am convinced that most parents would similarly abandon spanking if they knew how to replace it with promising alternatives and could experience the superior results firsthand. For those parents who are willing to move away from corporal punishment, positive alternatives are provided below.

Use a Behavioral Management System

Behavior management used to be called *behavior modification*. Basically it means *to use the laws of learning*, developed by such psychologists as B. F. Skinner, to change behavior. Stripped bare of all their theoretical and research complexities, the laws of learning are pretty simple and easy to master. They can be grouped into three areas, *classical conditioning, operant conditioning,* and *observational learning*:

Classical conditioning simply is the name given to the first type of learning, discovered by Ivan Pavlov. It deals with reflexive, or involuntary, behaviors only. If a stimulus (something that can be sensed such as a noise, smell, etc.) is paired with anything that causes a reflexive reaction, then an organism will start responding to that stimulus. For instance, with Pavlov's dog, the stimulus was a bell. It was paired with meat, so the dog started to salivate to the sound of the bell.

Most human emotional reactions have a conditioned component to them. Conditioned reactions will always occur whether we want them to or not. They are involuntary and automatic. We have no control and no choice, unless we understand them and deliberately expose ourselves to counterconditioning. An example would be *phobias*. Phobias attest to the power of this type of learning. Most people have a phobic response to something like snakes, heights, or flying. Everyone has conditioned emotional reactions to many things, such as the sound of a dentist's drill or a nostalgic song. Psychologists have a ninety-plus percent success rate in treating phobias using counterconditioning procedures. This law of learning is behind a number of the adverse side effects of punishment such as masochism, suppression, and negative emotional affect. The feelings of fear, anxiety, and alienation occur when we associate the punisher with the pain he induced. Extreme examples illustrate how this law affects behavior that is punished. Everyone has come into contact with an animal, like a dog, that fears men or children due to being abused at one time by a man or child. The dog has acquired a fear, or alienated response, to the stimulus associated with its pain. Oftentimes it will growl, nip, or bite at the feared person. A woman who has been raped, or sexually abused, may fear men for a long time afterwards or maybe even forever. Men who have been abused in childhood by their mothers acquire an emotionally conditioned response of hatred toward women which may later be expressed through the exploitation of women, domestic violence or—heaven forbid—serial killings. For sub-abusive physical punishment, the emotional response may not be as powerful as the above examples, but the laws of learning dictate that there absolutely will be some kind of negative emotional response. For this reason, the first principle of a good behavior management system is to avoid the use of physical punishment and minimize the use of all punishment. If it must be used, use it as a last resort, and use response cost. An example of *response cost* would be to punish a child for hitting his sister by requiring him to take out the trash (see next section).

The second type of learning, *operant conditioning*, is the most familiar. Stripped to its barest essentials, it means the use of reward and punishment. This is the heart of a good behavior management system, especially the reward part. When Skinner saw how negatively his rats responded to the use of punishment in his experiments, he came to realize it caused more problems than it solved and he discouraged its use. Punishment should be de-emphasized and again, when used, consist of response cost, particularly natural consequences (see below).

A good behavior management system to start off with, particularly with young children, is a *token economy*. The term *token economy* is used because this system is common in institutions such as psychiatric and mental retardation facilities, where the staff gives poker chips to clients, instead of money, for desired behaviors. The chips act as money. The clients collect them and cash them in later for rewards like privileges or food items at a commissary. Since clients are positively reinforced with a poker chip for desired behaviors, they learn to engage in them more frequently in order to get the rewards.

When implemented in the home, a checklist on the side of the refrigerator will suffice. The checklist should be prepared during a family meeting. It is best to have a prepared list of chores and give the kids a choice as to which chores they want to be responsible for. This avoids a reactance response and their participation in the decision-making makes them more committed to their choices because they willingly chose their chores rather than having them forced upon them. The kids should also participate in choosing the consequences for doing, or not doing, their chores. The deadline for completing chores each day and the inspection time should be made clear. A successfully-completed chore should be reinforced with a positive comment from the parent and recorded with a check mark placed in the proper box on the checklist. Check marks provide feedback to the kids. They always know where they stand. Parents have a record of progress, or lack thereof. Consequences should be specified for varying levels of success. If Junior successfully completes his chores three out of five days, he gets to go to the movies on Saturday. For four successful days, he gets to go swimming, etc. It is important to let the kids participate in picking the rewards because they must be attractive to them or they will not work.

Notice how this system emphasizes the positive. Where's the punishment? There really is none, and none should ever be necessary, if the system is implemented early and is used so consistently it becomes second nature. The reason no punishments are necessary is due to the fact that children want to please their parents more than anything else in the world. If they are praised daily for doing what their parents want, and they are crystal clear about what their parents want them to do, they will be more motivated to engage in those behaviors than anything else. Richard Miller and his colleagues (1975) conducted a study that clearly shows the superiority of using a positive approach to behavior. They had teachers try two different approaches to getting their students to keep the classroom clean of litter. Teachers in one class repeatedly told the kids they should be neat and tidy. This increased the amount of litter placed in the trash from 15% to 45%, but the effect did not last very long. By contrast, in another, similar class, the students were repeatedly congratulated by being told they were neat and tidy. Their level of cleanliness increased from 15% to 80% and persisted throughout the two weeks of the study.

Experimental evidence like this provides good evidence that a positive approach is superior to a negative one, as in authoritarian parenting, where the child is told to "Clean up your room or you'll get a good spanking."

A behavior management system gives children some control, which will minimize their resistance and help them acquire life skills. Parents may argue, "I'm the parent and I should be in control." The beauty is that you *are* in control, perhaps for the first time. You are using behavioral technology to get the behavior you want out of your child. One hundred years of behavioral science research has shown that there is no more effective way on the face of the earth to get what you want from others than by using behavior management techniques. One reason it works so well is because its a win-win situation. Perhaps for the first time, Junior also has control of his own destiny, which inspires loyalty to the system. It facilitates his learning to think for himself and learn how to monitor and manage his own behavior. He got to participate in the formulation of the system and feels a commitment to it. He got to chose his own rewards so he will be highly motivated to do what is necessary to obtain them. He gets constant reinforcement and always knows what the rules and consequences are. He has the power to get what he wants, and above all, has the security of always knowing what is expected and where he stands. There is no uncertainty or arbitrary punishments. Junior can feel the sense of accomplishment each week by seeing all the filled-in check marks and he feels good about himself. He has high self-esteem due to a sense of accomplishment made salient by the visible record of progress (check marks) and resultant rewards. Mom and Dad are relieved, too. They do not have to yell and scream or spank Junior all the time because he's not doing what he is supposed to do.

The third major learning theory, *observational learning,*

refers to imitating what others do. The expression, "Do as I say, not as I do" applies here. Most people realize that children are much more likely to imitate what their parents do rather than conform to what they say. This theory explains some of the adverse side effects of punishment such as aggression and imitating other undesirable behaviors of the model (the person the learner is imitating). Its role in behavior management is for the parents to act as a role model for desirable behaviors and avoiding modeling undesirable behaviors such as hitting, screaming, name-calling, demanding, or belittling. Again, using a behavior management system models the desirable behaviors of cooperation, respect, problem solving, planning, and responsibility.

This basic principle of behavior management—make the rules and consequences clear, give choices, and keep a record—will work for not only chores, but also in correcting all types of other behavior problems. Human behavior, being as complex as it is, takes advantage of every opportunity to create complications. Therefore, if parents have difficulty with a behavior management system, they should seek out additional resources such as books specializing in behavior management techniques or enroll in one of the many fine available parenting classes such as Parent Effectiveness Training (Gordon, 2000), Systematic Training for Effective Parenting, known as S.T.E.P. (Dinkmeyer & McKay, 1997), Effective Parenting (effectiveparenting.org), or Positive Parenting (positiveparenting.org).

Use Positive Reinforcement (praise) and Nonreinforcement (ignoring)

The best discipline strategy will minimize the use of punishment. Punishment is the last thing you want to use. It is best to use it as little as possible—only when it is absolutely necessary, which should not be very often, if you are putting enough emphasis on the positive behaviors. The real key to good behavior in children is to reinforce desirable behavior and not reinforce (ignore) undesirable behavior. As B. F. Skinner's students put it, "Spare the rod, use behavior mod!" The best way of eliminating bad behavior is to remove the rewarding consequences that sustains it. Problem behavior is often engaged in by children to get adult attention. For instance, the behavior of a child who is tantruming can best be eliminated not by punishment, but by not paying attention to the behavior and never giving in to the child's demands. This is called nonreinforcement, or ignoring the behavior.

Using nonreinforcement to extinguish undesirable behaviors can sometimes be difficult to achieve. It is hard to ignore a child who is constantly trying to interrupt while you are talking on the phone or who is clobbering a sibling. You cannot ignore a teenager who spends all day in front of the TV, rather than doing his homework, because watching TV is rewarding to him. In cases like these the parent has to set limits on the undesirable behavior and encourage those behaviors that are incompatible. For instance, you may set a limit for TV-watching time to one hour per day. Ignore Junior when he pleas for just one more hour. Then combine the extinction of TV watching with the reinforcement of alternative activities such as playing outdoors. You could even be very clever and use the Premack Principle, which is rewarding a less desirable behavior with a more desirable one. That is, use the permission to watch one hour of TV as a reward to Junior for completing his homework assignments. Instead of punishing a child for not cleaning up his room by grounding him, use negative reinforcement by saying he cannot come out of his room to play until it is cleaned up.

Another thing that is important to take into consideration when using nonreinforcement is the reason behind an undesirable behavior. Knowing the reason someone is acting up can act as a guide to an effective response. For instance, Junior may be acting out by saying four-letter words because he is suffering from lack of attention and is willing to put up with the negative attention of punishment as opposed to the anguish of getting no attention at all. Theoretically, ignoring Junior should eventually extinguish his use of four-letter words. But by not dealing with the root cause of Junior's acting out behaviors, the parent will then have to deal with the symptom substitution problem. That is, Junior will simply continue to act out in other ways, even if the use of bad words is ignored and extinguished, by experimenting with other problem behaviors. He will act out in other ways until he gets a rise out of Mom and eventually collects the fruit of his acting out, some kind of attention, albeit negative in nature. This whole scenario could be avoided if the parent took the time to do a little troubleshooting and realized Junior is crying out for attention. The attention should be provided, in conjunction with the nonreinforcement of using four-letter words, in order to arrive at a definitive solution to Junior's acting out problem.

Use Subtractive Punishment (time-out, loss of privileges)

Psychologists define punishment as *any event that decreases the probability of a response* and they classify all forms of physical punishment under the rubric of *additive punishment*. Additive punishment (sometimes called positive punishment, which is a term I do not like to use because it is confusing in the sense that it makes it sound like it is a good thing to do which it is not) is one of two types of punishment: It is defined as *introducing an intrinsically painful stimulus*. Spanking, hitting, shoving, slapping, verbal abuse, and screaming at someone are all types of *additive punishment*.

The other type of punishment, which is much more desirable, and the one psychologists recommend be used instead of spanking, is called *subtractive punishment* (the removal of a pleasant stimulus). The classic example is *time-out. Grounding* is the teenage equivalent of time-out. One problem that parents encounter when using a time-out chair is that young children tend to get up and run around rather than sit it the chair for the two or three minutes of time-out. Roberts (1990) recommends that mothers escort noncompliant children to their bedrooms, where they sit for a few minutes. They are then taken back to the time-out chair. Repeating this process a few times may be necessary but it was effective in getting children to sit in the time-out chair for the required two or three minute time-out. Time-outs are good for breaking out of a negative cycle. They allow everyone to take a break, think calmly, and try again later.

Subtractive punishment (so called because something desired is removed) can consist of revoking any privilege. Revoking TV watching, driving privileges, or dessert are all common forms of subtractive punishment. Technically, both types of punishment will elicit the thirteen undesirable side effects, but additive punishment does so to a much greater degree. That is why it is best, while disciplining, to emphasize rewards rather than punishment. However, if punishment must be used, subtractive punishment is superior to additive punishment because it minimizes the occurrence of the negative side effects.

Skeptical parents may declare, "Losing privileges won't work. What that child needs is a good spanking!" Consider an incident that I heard the other day. A colleague was relaying a disciplinary episode he had just experienced at home: His eight-year-old son lost his Nintendo playing privileges for two days for coming home late from school. The boy drove his parents crazing by begging for a spanking instead because that punishment would be over immediately and he could resume playing his beloved Nintendo games. Which punishment looks more effective now? While a spanking is over immediately, revoking a privilege gives a child many hours to contemplate the wisdom of his transgression.

Use Response Cost

Response cost involves paying a higher cost in time, effort, and inconvenience than the forbidden behavior gains. For instance, if a child rides her bike without a helmet, what has she gained? She's saved a few minutes of time and inconvenience by skipping the safety step of putting on her helmet before going on a bike ride. When caught, her mother does not have to yell or get angry if she uses response cost. She can simply require her daughter to "pay" for her transgression by doing something more onerous, like scrubbing the kitchen floor. After a while the daughter will learn that it is a lot easier to put on her bicycle helmet than to scrub the kitchen floor.

It is also important to understand some basic psychological theory to act as a guide to effective discipline. One day after lecturing a class on learning theory, classical conditioning, operant conditioning, and observational learning, a student approached me after class and said, "All this theory is well and good, Dr. Marshall, but how can it help me solve the problem of my ex-boyfriend refusing to leave me alone after I broke off my relationship with him?" She went on to explain that her ex continued to call her late into the night, not allowing her to get her needed sleep. If she disconnected the phone, he would simply drive over and continue to knock on her door or window until she would accede to his request of "Just talk to me for ten minutes and then I'll leave you alone and let you get to sleep."

Further probing revealed that her relationship started out

in the typical way, very romantic and exciting. She thought he was Mr. Wonderful and couldn't wait, in the beginning, to see and be close to him. After a few months of dating, she fell in love with him and was anxious to please him, so she happily offered to make his apartment rent payment for him when he lost his job. She didn't want him to end up homeless and sleeping in the streets. He was so grateful, he told her he'd love her forever and pay her back as soon as he got another job. She was also willing to help him out financially when his car payment, insurance, and utility bills came due. Of course, he would pay her back when he got a job. Being unemployed made him a little depressed so she would further help him out by cleaning up his apartment, buying groceries, fixing his dinner, and washing his clothes.

He was also a little self-centered, but she didn't mind so much because she was in love with him. On his birthday, she would phone him to say how much she loved him, give him a card and present, and bake a cake for the surprise party she would throw for him. When it was her birthday, she would wait by the phone all day hoping to hear from him, only to fall asleep crying in disappointment that he never called or acknowledged her birthday. He also had a bad habit of being late for dates, even though she had to pay for the gas, dinner, and movie. By now, he owed her over $10,000.00 and he was having trouble finding a job. But all of this was okay with her because she loved him.

"Then why did you break up with him?" I asked. The straw that broke the camel's back, she explained, occurred one night when he was four hours late coming over to her house to pick her up for a date. She was so worried, she phoned his apartment to see if something had happened to him. When she got no answer she became frantic and called the police and hospitals to try to locate him, thinking he must surely be in trouble.

When the phone calls failed to locate him, she decided to search for him in her car. She drove to his apartment first and knocked. Although no one answered, she could hear noise inside. Having a key, she entered, only to find him in a compromising position with another woman. Furious, she screamed that it was over, that she never wanted to see him again, and stormed off. That's when the bugging behavior started. He was happy with the relationship, for obvious reasons, and was highly motivated to continue it. His goal was to keep contacting her until he could talk her into continuing the relationship. Besides, he needed her. Another car payment had come due.

She was in quite a quandary. She wanted to know how she could get him to quit bugging her. She said she tried everything and the bugging behavior only got worse with time. I was able to assist her in translating class theory into practice. We were able to immediately put her knowledge of the laws of learning to work to help her solve her problem with his behavior. First off she had to realize that she was reinforcing his bugging behavior and that is what was sustaining it. Every time she gave in to his demand to talk to him "for just ten minutes" so he would leave her alone, she reinforced him with the attention of talking to him. If she had never given in from the beginning (nonreinforcement), his bugging behavior would have eventually extinguished because it was not getting him anything useful. To make matters worse, she was reinforcing him in the worse possible way—with partial reinforcement.

B. F. Skinner, the eminent learning psychologist, made a brilliant discovery, by serendipity, about behavior in the 1950's while conducting his rat studies. Previously he had invented the Skinner Box, which he called an *operant conditioning chamber*. It was an automated cage for rats which allowed him to conduct multiple studies simultaneously by collecting data on many rats at a time. Before his invention, psychologists had to watch the rat constantly, reinforce it every time it exhibited the desired behavior, and record events in a data-collection notebook. Skinner designed his box to automatically send a food pellet down a chute into a food dish when the rat pressed a bar and record the rats bar-pressing response electronically on an event recorder that kept a running total of its responses, much like the long strip of paper used by seismologists to record earthquakes.

One day Skinner entered his lab, only to find a food chute was jamming in one of his Skinner boxes, and sending down a food pellet not for every bar press, but for only some. In other words, the rat may have to press the bar five times, versus once, to get one food pellet. At first Skinner thought it was a catastrophe, that his experiment was ruined because of the jammed-food mechanism, but he noticed something peculiar. The rat was bar-pressing faster than any rat he had ever seen. Then the notion struck him, he had discovered something momentous about behavior, something that could benefit every person in the world operating a business. *He found a way to get more work for less pay.* That's right, the rat was willing to press the bar five times (work) for one food pellet (pay), instead of only once per food pellet, *and the rat was working faster than ever before.* He was getting five times as much work out of the rat for one food pellet as he did before he chanced upon this bit of serendipitous luck.

He immediately wanted to find out exactly how powerful this effect was, that is, how much work could he possibly get for one little payment, a food pellet. He decided to test pigeons, training them to peck a key (as in a typewriter type of key) in a cage with continuous reinforcement (one kernel of corn for each key peck). Then he started to cut back. One kernel for two pecks, three pecks, four pecks, etc. How many pecks do you think the pigeon was willing to give for one kernel before it gave up, or in human terms, went on strike and refused to peck the key anymore, due to insufficient pay? If you guessed 700 pecks you were right. That's a lot of work for very little pay! Further studies revealed that when animals were trained using partial reinforcement, it took much longer to extinguish their behavior using nonreinforcement. Psychologists call this *persistence training.*

This is all well and good when talking about animal behavior, but that doesn't mean it holds true with humans, you may be thinking. Let me provide you with a little labor-law history. After entering the port of New York at the turn of the century, immigrants regularly obtained one of their first jobs in the new world in the garment industry. Owners would save overhead money by giving fabric to their workers to take home and sew into clothes. That way business owners did not have to bear the expense of buying and maintaining factory floor space for their workers to work in. This practice was known as "homework." The immigrants, or any other employee, might sew together 100 shirts, for instance, and then bring them back to the boss for payment and pick up the next batch of fabric to bring home to sew. In essence, this is a system of paying workers with partial reinforcement. The worker sews together a shirt and doesn't get any payment for it. She sews another, no payment, and another, etc. until she has sewn 100 shirts, still with no payment for all her work. When she drops them off with her boss, in a batch, in the garment district, he will then reinforce her with one check for the 100 times she sewed shirts together with no payment. This is a partial schedule of 100 to one. The worker was willing to do 100 pieces of work for one payment. Although it's not exactly the same situation as with the pigeon or rat (the worker gets a bigger payment in the end while the rat's payment remains constant), it has the same effect. Labor unions became so alarmed at how much work the immigrants were willing to do for such a small amount of pay, that they successfully lobbied Congress to outlaw this type of work arrangement under the argument that it was exploitative of the worker. They were right in terms of its ability to exploit. When paid on a partial schedule, just like the pigeons, immigrants were willing to work up to 18 hours a day, seven days a week, year round, for less than subsistence pay.

What does all of this have to do with my student's ex-boyfriend problem? You may already see the connection. By her hanging up on him again and again, only to eventually give in and talk to him on the phone for ten minutes so he'd fulfill his promise to leave her alone to go to sleep, she was reinforcing him with her attention on a partial schedule. This had a dual impact on his behavior, both of them undesirable. It increased the level at which he would bug her (more frequently) and also meant he would be much more persistent at it (continue to bug her long after she stopped reinforcing him). In other words, he was willing to do more work (dial her number) for less pay (her attention). His persistence at pressing the phone button sounds eerily similar to Skinner's pigeon pecking the Skinner Box key.

When the underlying psychological dynamics of the situation became clear to her, she was horrified at what she had been doing. Due to her incomplete understanding of the psychology of learning, she was actually *throwing gasoline on the fire*, so to speak, by responding to him in such a way as to make his behavior worse. Why was she so willing to give in to him? The other side of the coin is that she was getting something out of it too. Her giving-in behavior increased because it was reinforced in another way, called *negative reinforcement*. Negative reinforcement is often confused with punishment. It is not punishment. It is different, for punishment decreases the frequency of a behavior, while positive and negative reinforcement both increase the frequency of a behavior. The difference is that with punishment a painful stimulus is introduced while with positive reinforcement a pleasant stimulus is introduced. Slapping someone is punishment because it is painful. Someone who gets slapped for saying something will likely say it less in order to avoid the painful consequence. Alternatively, if a child were given an M&M candy for putting a toy away in the closet, she would be very likely to put another toy away in the closet in order to receive the pleasant consequence of getting candy.

The way in which negative reinforcement differs is that it provides something positive too—it stops pain. If your fingers got slammed in the car door, wouldn't it feel wonderful to open the door and relieve the painful pressure of the door crushing them? The act of opening the door was reinforced. It got something nice for the victim. It got him relief from pain. The pain is the "negative" part in negative reinforcement. What is done to get rid of it is the behavior that is reinforced. It will increase in frequency because it worked—it got relief. In the same way my student was getting relief. She continually gave in to her ex and talked to him because she was able to get relief from the incessant calling and was able to get to sleep. She was negatively reinforced for talking to him, so she did it again and again.

Negative reinforcement is an insidious trap for parents who are trying to effectively discipline their children. Imagine a parent who is in the supermarket checkout line: She has a four-year-old who has picked up a pack of gum, conveniently placed at the child's eye level by clever marketers. The child keeps nagging Momma to buy it. Momma says no and tries to concentrate on the scanner prices, hoping to catch an error and receive a free food item. The child is persistent. He keeps nagging, whining, and tugging on Momma's clothes, insistent that she buy the gum for him. Momma's getting increasingly irritated. She has had a hectic day at work, fought traffic on the commute home, paid a fine for picking up Junior late at the day care center, fought the crowds in the supermarket aisles, dreads the thought of having to go home, fix dinner, and wash the clothes, and has a pounding headache to boot. She can't take it anymore. She wants to stop Junior now. In learning terms, she has only three choices: She can smack Junior to shut him up (punishment), she can ignore him (nonreinforcement), or, she can give in to him (negative reinforcement). Say she chooses to give in to him and says "all right, get the gum." Junior immediately shuts up. He's happy as a clam. Did Momma get what she wanted? You bet. She got relief. She was negatively reinforced. It worked. According to learning theory, she's going to do it again because that giving-in behavior was reinforced for her. The outcome feels good to her and seems to work.

Avoid Reinforcing Undesirable Behaviors

Was it a good solution? Let's examine the situation from Junior's perspective. What did he learn? He learned that being a brat is a good thing for him. It gets him what he wants. He was positively reinforced (with gum) by Momma for acting like a brat. He's going to do it again and again. Poor Momma! She's in a real bind. Unless she understands the psychology of learning, she may never realize that there is a powerful unconscious force increasing the frequency of her ineffective parenting behaviors—negative reinforcement. When these two learning concepts are put together, partial and negative reinforcement, a powerful principle of effective parenting emerges—consistency.

Dr. Gerald Patterson, a clinical psychologist and research director of the Oregon Social Learning Center in Eugene,

Oregon, is an expert on childhood aggression. He explains how children who have serious behavioral problems, such as Oppositional Defiant Disorder, are the products of inconsistent parenting. What typically goes wrong is that when a child refuses to comply with the parents' wishes, they back down because the child's tantrums and whining wear them down. It is much easier to give up than pursue the battle. That only acts to reinforce the child's oppositional pattern. The parents may initially counter the child's opposition by yelling, getting angry, and threatening, but rarely follow through on their threats. Ultimately, what the child has learned is that whining, yelling and tantruming get you what you want. These become a substitute social skill. Parents who consistently apply consequences are going to avoid the above problems. Keep in mind that the consequence to an undesirable behavior may be *nothing*, that is, ignoring the child (nonreinforcement). If that's your choice, then remember to never give in and your child will not be reinforced on a partial schedule for undesirable behavior, and you will not be negatively reinforced by giving in and won't end up creating a spoiled brat. Consequences other than nonreinforcement can be used, too. In fact, natural consequences are the best kind to use.

Use Natural Consequences

Many a parent has argued with their child over dressing warmly to go outside to play in the winter. Consider the following scenario:

Parent: "Put your coat on. It's cold outside."
Child: "I don't need it."
Parent: "Put your coat on or you'll catch a cold."
Child: "I can't find my coat."

Parent: "Put your coat on, I said!"
Child: "Why do I have to wear my coat?"
Parent: "Because I said so."
Child: "No. I don't want to!"

This is a battle that is totally unnecessary, not to mention the fact that being cold has nothing to do with catching a cold. Natural consequences are completely sufficient to deal with this situation. Simply let Junior go out in the cold without his coat. Very shortly he will be back, shivering, and searching the house diligently for his coat. This is the power of natural consequences. It makes life much easier. There are fewer battles, less aggravation, and no more power struggles.

Modeling Desirable Behaviors

Albert Bandura's studies demonstrated how powerful is the impact adult behavior has on children. By mere passive observation, children are virtually compelled to imitate adult behavior. If they imitate the aggressive behavior they witness at home and on television, then we would expect them to also imitate any positive adult behavior they observe. Parents can harness the power of observational learning by modeling such positive behavioral traits as patience, respect, kindness, cooperation, and empathy. Children should never be attacked, put down, belittled, ridiculed, deliberately embarrassed, or punished in front of friends. Respect is a critical ingredient for all successful human relationships. Before parents can expect to receive it from their children, they must first model how it is done in the way they treat them.

Stop the Screaming and Yelling

Screaming, yelling, and name-calling are not a good substitute for physical punishment. They are just another type of punishment. It may be verbal rather than physical, but it hurts just as much. Consequently, many of the adverse side effects of physical punishment occur with verbal punishment as well. The kids will just fear and avoid their parents. Furthermore, the children grow up learning to deal with interpersonal problems in the same ineffective and damaging way as that modeled by their parents.

Parents are trained by their kids to yell louder and more often in a vicious, and never-ending, escalating cycle, through the process of negative reinforcement. When the parent first screams, it gets the kids' attention. Mom or Dad is now satisfied (reinforced) in two different ways: First, they have vented their emotion, which releases a little bit of their pent-up tension, and secondly, they have captured their kids' attention. Soon, however, the children adapt to the incessant yelling and tune it out. Guess what Mom and Dad have to do now to recapture their kids' attention? How can parents break out of this destructive pattern? A behavioral technique called self-monitoring works well. Parents need to record what is happening so they can recognize and correct it. Every time a yelling incident occurs, the parent needs to write down four things. (1) The antecedent—that is, what triggered the incident. (2) The behavioral response of the parent, such as screaming, hitting, throwing an object, name-calling, etc. (3) The consequence, such as feeling bad, guilty, unsatisfied, or the kids crying, etc. (4) Where and when the incident took place—that is, the time and place.

Some very powerful things happen when people take the time to collect this type of data on their behavior: First, they become aware of it. Most of our daily behavior is habitual. It is so automatic and unthinking that we are not fully aware of what we are doing. Once we write it down, we can readily see what is happening. This puts us in a position to analyze it and come up with solutions using problem-solving techniques. Step one of problem-solving is to state the problem. A careful examination of the data should reveal where the problems are: For instance, does a cluster of yelling involve getting the kids off to school on time? Step two is to generate possible solutions: Would setting their bedtime earlier or making sure chores and homework get done earlier so the kids get to bed earlier help? What about cutting caffeine out of their diet so they fall asleep more easily at bedtime? What about preparing lunches and laying out clothes the night before to prevent being rushed and stressed in the morning? Step three is to pick some of the most promising possible solutions and implement them. And of course, step four is to evaluate the effectiveness of whatever solution was attempted. If it is not working, go back through the process again until an effective solution is discovered.

Another way to get a handle on this type of destructive pattern is to record the problem incidents on a videotape recorder and view it with the same type of problem-solving attitude. Chances are you will discover yourself saying or doing something foolish or destructive of which you were not even aware. Some solutions may be obvious. If the kids are poking and antagonizing each other in the back car seat or at the dinner table, a situational solution would be in order. Just separate the children. Put one in the front and the other in back or seat them out of range of each other at the dinner table.

Yelling, screaming, anger, and rage are always a symptom of ineffective communication. In the same way that we will increase the volume of our question when talking to a foreigner who didn't understand what we said the first time, we begin to yell at our family members when we feel we are not getting through to them. Another way to break the yelling cycle is to think about what we want to say before yelling. Take a time out for yourself, and deal with the situation later when you've calmed down. Remember to use the "two eyes" technique, eye contact and "I" messages. Looking at a child right in the eyes does two things: It gets their attention so we know they are listening and it makes it harder for us to yell at them because they are more humanized. We can readily see that this is a child. The "I" messages should express what emotion we are experiencing. Instead of "You idiot! How could you ride your bike in front of that car? You almost got killed! You're too irresponsible to ride a bike. Come inside now. You can't play anymore. You're grounded." Say: "*I* was scared to death. *I* am so relieved you're okay. *I* need you to ride your bike more carefully. My nerves can't take much more of this. You know what the rules are about riding in the street. Your bike gets put away for three days."

The second message is very different from the first. It was a more honest communication, rather than an attempt at domination, power, and control. The mother used natural consequences. She is not the bad guy because they had taken the time to previously discuss and make up a set of rules. The rules and consequences were clearly communicated and known to everyone. They had a system. No egos were involved. Junior has no ill will toward his mother. She didn't yell, name call, or attack him. She didn't even really punish him. The system was responsible for taking the bike away. She was not excited or emotionally involved in the consequences. Her only emotional concern was for Junior's safety. His self-esteem was not jeopardized. There's no need to tell him he's irresponsible. Consistent consequences will teach him how to be responsible. Since he's motivated to get his bike back and not lose it again, he'll automatically learn to act responsibly next time to avoid the consequences. He feels no resentment toward his mother and has no need to get defensive, counterattack, or retaliate.

He feels good that mom cares so much about his safety. He feels what happened was fair since he knew about the rules and consequences in advance. There were no surprises or arbitrary punishments. There's no battle of wills, power struggles, or ego involvement. The neutral behavior management "system" is in operation and has successfully dealt with the situation as planned. Communication skills are the foundation upon which effective discipline is built.

Use Communication Skills

True communication involves allowing others the freedom to speak whatever is on their mind without interruption or judgment. Families that lack good communication suffer from either inappropriate or interrupted communication. Inappropriate communication involves name calling, sarcasm, or criticism. Calling kids "stupid," "lazy," or "bad" creates a breeding ground for poor communication because they will learn to talk back to adults in kind. Too often parents interrupt their children's communication because they have learned how to communicate inappropriately by—guess who—the parents themselves. Saying, "You idiot, why did you tell my friends I flunked the driver's test!" is inappropriate. Children need to be able to deal directly with their frustration, anger, and resentment. If they can't, then they will act them out in inappropriate ways. It is the parents' job to teach their children how to deal effectively with their emotions. If parents model respectful communication, then the children will learn to express themselves more appropriately as in, "Dad, you embarrassed me in front of my friends when you told them I flunked my driver's test."

Gordon (2000) believes one of the biggest mistakes parents make is to cut off their children's feelings and emotions through interruptive communication statements. For instance, a crying daughter might say, "I flunked my algebra test. I'll never be any good at math!" The natural tendency is to try to make the child feel better by saying, "There, there now, don't cry. It's only one test. You're perfectly fine at math." According to Gordon, this cuts off the child's feelings by interrupting her grief. She needs to be allowed to go through the feelings first before she can think rationally about a solution. What she really needs at the time is empathy. She needs to know that her feelings are legitimate and someone is there for her, not someone that will interrupt her emotions and interfere with her emotional healing process.

Yes, humans are rational creatures, but thank goodness, we are also emotional creatures. We need to learn to express and deal with the full range of emotions, both good and bad. When allowed to experience their emotions, people will amazingly exit the other side of their emotions by becoming rational and thinking of their own solutions. They cannot be rushed. They will be amenable to rational solutions only when they are ready for them. That's after they have been allowed to process their emotions, which can only happen if they are given the time and space needed to experience them. It's difficult to put this concept into practice because parents automatically want to protect their kids from emotional pain.

My daughter came home from her new middle school one day crying, "Nobody likes me. I don't have any friends." I immediately began to comfort her with, "That's not true. You have lots of friends." Her response to my approach was irritation at the fact that I did not understand what she was talking about and to argue with me and "prove" that she was right by giving examples of how she was rejected during the day. At some point I realized my approach was not working and changed course. When I put my arms around her and said, "I know, sweetheart. It's hard to be accepted at a new school," she started crying all the harder and cried for a long time. I didn't say a word. I just let her cry it out. Finally, she said, "Thanks, Dad. I love you." The interesting part is that my second approach was much easier than the first. I didn't have to come up with all kinds of solutions and argue with her about why she wouldn't be reasonable and accept my perfectly good solutions. All I had to do was listen, acknowledge, and empathize with her. The next evening she ran up to me when I got home from work. She was all chipper. She exclaimed, "Daddy, I've got an idea. I'm going to start my own "in" group. There's a lot of kids like me who don't know anyone. We'll be each other's friends." She was perfectly able to come up with her own rational solution to the problems, but only after she was given the chance to work through the emotional process. Facilitating the ability of children to identify and talk about their feelings raises their emotional IQ and will improve their chances of success in life (Goleman, 1995). Children who can talk about their feelings will be much less likely to act them out in misbehavior.

Good communication techniques also emphasize the positive and teach the child while disciplining. It is important to avoid name-calling. Indict the behavior, not the child. Instead of saying, "You liar," say, "If you do not tell the truth about borrowing your sister's outfit, she will not trust you and be unlikely to trade clothes with you in the future." Use a discipline opportunity to teach correct behaviors, including being a good role model for how to treat others with respect. Rather than saying, "Shut up, you wild animals!" say "Please be quiet or go outside and play. I need to concentrate on paying the bills."

Do Not Reinforce a Behavior a Child Naturally Likes

One word of caution is in order on the use of rewards. Try to never reinforce a child for good behavior that she enjoys and would do anyway, even if no reward were given. The reason for this is that a reward can destroy the pleasure of doing something for its own sake. There is ample research evidence to support this notion. In one experiment, children were given magic markers and blank paper to draw on during play time (Lepper, Greene, & Nisbett, 1973). Not surprisingly, they liked this activity. However, half the children were rewarded for this activity with a "Good Player Award." The other half of the children were not led to expect a reward and were not given one. One week later the experimenters gave both groups of children another opportunity to play with the magic markers and paper. Children in the rewarded group spent much less time playing with the felt-tip pens than those who were not rewarded. By contrast, the unrewarded group showed just as much interest in the activity as they had shown in their free play time before the experiment had begun. Why did these surprising results occur? Remember our old friend from Chapter 3, the self-justification effect? The children who were rewarded for playing with the magic markers came to believe that the reason they must have been playing with the magic markers was because of the external reward they received after doing it. By contrast, the unrewarded children had only one reasonable explanation for their behavior—they must have played with the markers because they found it enjoyable, not because they were rewarded for doing so.

This lesson is illustrated in the story of the clever old man whose solitude was being disturbed by rowdy children. One day he approached the children with an offer, "I like to hear you play," he said. "If you come here and make lots of noise each day I'll pay you a quarter. " The children gladly accommodated the old man. But the next day he told them he was short on cash and could only pay them twenty cents each. Although the children were a little disappointed, they accepted his offer. Each day the old man offered them a nickel less than the day before. On the fifth day, when the offer had dwindled to a nickel, the children indignantly refused to make noise for only five cents. "It's not worth it," they snorted, and promptly ran off, leaving the man to enjoy his newfound tranquillity.

I have applied these research findings in how I reward my own children. All of my kids play soccer. They find playing the game intrinsically rewarding, especially making goals. I have observed that many of the soccer players' parents pay their kids money for each goal their son or daughter makes during games. Upon hearing about this potential gold mine, my children approached me with the proposition that I, too, pay them for making goals like the other parents do. I politely declined by replying that scoring a goal is its own reward, even more pleasing than making a few dollars. Although they did not like my explanation, they never lost the thrill of scoring soccer goals through their years of playing soccer. The same thing occurred with other intrinsically rewarding activities like making "A's" on their report cards and reading books. Whenever they asked to get paid like their friends did for these activities, I always refused to do so.

What all this shows is that extrinsically rewarded behavior is more temporary in quality than intrinsically rewarded behavior. That does not mean that rewards should never be used. They are best used on those activities that are tedious, such as skill-building exercises. For instance, copious rewards, such as praise, can be very effective in teaching a child how to sound out words or swing a bat. The short-term effectiveness of extrinsic rewards is appropriate for these types of situations. However, once the skill has been acquired, and the activity becomes intrinsically rewarding, then the reinforcers should be phased out. Rewards work best when they are dispensed mainly for making progress (Deci, 1975).

Other Techniques that Can be Used Instead of Spanking

Family Development Resources (1990) recommends the following techniques in their parenting training course and video:

1. **Reward and Praise**. Take the time to catch your kids doing something right and praise them often. The laws of learning indicate that children will increase good behaviors when they are praised, thus crowding out the bad behaviors and replacing them with positive behaviors. Emphasizing positive behaviors builds your child's self-esteem. When children's behaviors are praised and encouraged, they are happier and more motivated to continue engaging in the praised behavior. A child who is constantly criticized and told that he is bad or can't do anything right becomes sullen and acquires low self-esteem. A happy child who feels good about himself is much easier to live with and manage. Children learn more about good behavior when they are told what they are doing right as opposed to what they do wrong. Don't forget to express affection regularly. Children thrive when parents emphasize how much they love them versus dwelling on every little thing they do wrong. Children need—first and foremost—to feel loved.

2. **Prevention**. Childproof the house. Put temptations out of sight and out of mind. For example, put latches on the cabinet that contains the cleaners and dangerous stuff. Leave one cabinet free for your child to open and play with the contents. Fill it with the safe plastic dinnerware and Tupperware.

3. **Redirection**. This is particularly appropriate for young children. For example, if your child is pulling on the curtains, bring her into another room and offer her paper and crayons to play with. Bad behavior will quickly end when a child can be distracted with a better alternative.

4. **Communicate**. Take time to find out why your child is not cooperating. Good communication involves listening to your child's feelings without condemning. For instance, if your child resists going to school, it may be because he has not completed his homework or a bully is picking on him and he has not mentioned it out of fear or humiliation.

5. **Establish clear rules and consequences in advance**. Children need to know the standards of behavior to follow. A chore list should be discussed in advance and posted so everyone can see it. For instance, if the child is expected to empty the trash daily by 6 P.M. and it is not done, then the TV may be turned off for the night. Likewise, other expectations like curfews and their consequences should be made clear in advance.

6. **Remove a privilege**. Time-out and loss of privileges should be used as a last resort. It is best to remove those that are related to the behavior. If your child leaves her bike in the middle of the sidewalk where someone could trip over it, for punishment she would lose her bike riding privileges for a few days.

7. **Give realistic choices and consequences**. Unrealistic threats such as "I'll knock your block off if you don't change clothes!" makes a parent lose credibility. Saying, "Son, you have a choice. You can leave your tank top on and we will not be able to go to the movies, or you can change into a tee shirt and we'll leave in ten minutes to go see a movie. What's your choice?"

8. **Use humor**. A child who is having fun is more likely to cooperate. Saying something funny like "If you don't put

your shoes away I'm going to eat your toes!" can also help to avoid power struggles.

9. **Give transition time**. Telling your child that dinner will be ready in thirty minutes, when he is playing basketball in the driveway with his friends, gives him time to finish his activity, thus teaching the lessons of good communication and respect for the activities of others, while avoiding the power struggle that goes along with demanding immediate obedience.

10. **Help your child**. A young child who is told to "clean up your room" can easily become overwhelmed. You can take the time to help her. If you make helping fun, you get a number of benefits such as spending quality time with your child, teaching cooperation, building trust, and teaching her how to clean properly by modeling the desired behavior.

Ways to Stop Spanking

What can parents, who are resolved to stop spanking, do to control themselves when they feel like doing so? First, as discussed earlier, parents should engage in some self-monitoring. They need to become aware of what triggers their anger and angry responses. It's best to keep a written record in a log of what situations provoke hitting a child. Once the triggers are identified, they can be dealt with using problem-solving techniques. For instance, if it's being bombarded with noise and kid-requests upon entering the door after a stressful day at work and jangled freeway nerves, then requesting help from a spouse, friend, relative, or baby-sitter to watch the kids so you can be left alone to unwind and relax for a half hour first, is a reasonable solution.

Self-help groups are wonderful and free of charge. Anyone can hook up with Parents Anonymous by simply calling the number listed in the phone book or logging on to parentsanonymous.org. They provide social support with group meetings, help in working through the twelve steps to self-control, and a sponsor or other members who can be called when needed.

Never spank because you are angry. Take a few minutes to gather your thoughts and cool off first. Call a support person to talk it out. Ask a spouse, relatives, neighbors, or sitters to take over and go somewhere to cool off. Count to ten. Exit the situation for a cooling off period by going into another room or going for a walk. Try a response incompatible with anger by hugging your child or using a humorous response to the situation. Use a cognitive defusing strategy such as saying to yourself, "Is this infraction really worth hurting my child?" or "Will this matter months from now?" Pat yourself on the back in advance for showing restraint. Call a national hotline such as 1-800-448-3000 for a Boy's Town counselor. Take parenting classes to learn about and practice alternatives to spanking. Experiment and find whatever alternative works for you. Above all, be patient. Remind yourself that children need lots of practice and repetition before they can understand what they are supposed to do and get it right. If you should make a mistake, don't be too hard on yourself. Nobody's perfect; parents are bound to make mistakes. Raising children can be extremely stressful at times. Anyone can be pushed beyond the breaking point. If you explode and lash out occasionally at your kids verbally, or possibly even shove or hit them, it's not the end of the world. Recognize that children are resilient and will survive it. You can help them, and yourself, get over the incident more quickly if you are willing to take responsibility for what you did and be honest about it. If you apologize to your child and tell her what you did was wrong, she not only will get over the incident much quicker, but she will also learn some important life-lessons about honesty and taking responsibility.

I want to end this chapter by making some general statements about good child-raising practices. It may appear at this point that my message is that if a child is spanked, she will grow up to be a monster and if she is not spanked, she will grow up to be a saint. Nothing could be further from the truth! My point is that *all other things being equal,* an individual parent will get better discipline results by using alternatives to spanking rather than by spanking. The reason for this clarification is because, obviously, a child who is raised in a very neglectful household, but is never spanked, will be much worse off than a child who is raised in a loving household but spanked occasionally when disciplined.

There are much more powerful forces that have an impact on a child's behavior while developing than whether or not she is spanked. The parenting dimensions that predict the highest level of psychosocial functioning in children are:

1. Closeness or Warmth—an emphasis on affection, nurturance, and acceptance of the child by the parent (Maccoby and Martin, 1983).
2. Control or monitoring—parental involvement in the child's life, supervision of the child's activities, and firmness in setting controls and limits (Patterson, 1982a).
3. Authoritative parents (combine limit-setting with warmth) vs. authoritarian (high on discipline, low on warmth)—The authoritative parenting style produces the most well-adjusted children (Baumrind, 1978).
4. Emotional control (managing one's own feelings well)— The ability to control impulses, delay gratification, persist in the face of frustrations, regulate one's moods, keep distress from swamping one's ability to think, the ability to empathize, and maintaining hope is a better predictor of success and happiness in life than IQ (Goleman, 1995; Myers, 1992).

Poor child management techniques are related to children's use of alcohol, cigarettes, marijuana, illicit drugs, and other acting-out and control problems (Dishion, Patterson, and Reid, 1988). Drug use in children is predicted by parental lack of affection, lack of acceptance of the child, detachment, poor discipline, weak or excessive controls, lack of supervision, and inconsistency. Occasional spanking is going to take a back seat to all of the above. That said, it is still true that the more a child is spanked, the more of the thirteen undesirable side effects a parent will have to contend with. These side effects fall along a continuum: Parents who use spanking minimally will impose on their children the fewest and weakest side effects. As the amount of spanking increases, so will the side effects. Those parents who rely upon spanking frequently for discipline will accrue the greatest burden of side effects.

We once lived in a condominium where there was a four-year-old neighbor boy who was Satan's curse on communal living. I'll call him Tommy (not his real name). He regularly threw rocks through windows, smashed bottles in the driveway, and urinated on the other kids—you get the picture. He was not a nice boy. One day we got home from the beach and we noticed that one of our condo windows was open. We remembered leaving it closed so we knew something was wrong. We inspected everything in the house very carefully and found that the only things missing were some of our son's toys. We immediately thought of Tommy and went outside looking for him. Sure enough, he was playing with my son's toys on the sidewalk in front of his unit. Naturally we informed his mother of what had transpired and she told us not to worry, she would teach him a lesson. As we got back into our living room we could hear her punishing little Tommy. She gave him the spanking of his life, screaming at him the whole time. As a matter of fact, she did the same thing the next time he got into trouble, and the next, and the next. It didn't take me long to realize what Tommy's problem *really* was; he was a classic case of a severe manifestation of the undesirable side effects of spanking. We moved soon afterward, but I have often wondered in the succeeding eighteen years what became of our little four-year-old burglar neighbor. I'm not sure I want to know the answer.

Chapter 6

A Word About Healthy Discipline

A key component of most parents' discipline strategy is punishment. And punishment has traditionally meant spanking. Today many informed parents are making the transition to noncorporal forms of punishment, such as time-out. This is a step in the right direction toward better childhood discipline practices. Parents who use time-out will never have to suffer through the agony of taking their child to the emergency room due to an accidental injury resulting from corporal punishment gone awry. However, time-out is still a form of punishment. It is subtractive (the removal of a pleasant stimulus). Unfortunately, the other 12 negative side effects of spanking can still occur when noncorporal punishment is used. They are just not as severe. Skinner (1976) recognized the undesirable side effects of punishment and advocated a society that was reinforcement-oriented in his book *Walden Two*. His vision of a utopian society has been implemented in a commune called Twin Oaks, located in Louisa, Virginia, which is still active today.

Skinner did not "approve" of the use of punishment, not out of ethical considerations, but on a pragmatic basis—he knew it doesn't work well. Skinner discovered that punishment only temporarily acts to interfere with whatever stimulus is reinforcing the undesired behavior. Until the positive reinforcer that sustains the behavior is removed the "bad" behavior will keep returning, in spite of the punishment. For instance, punishing Junior for teasing his sister will only temporarily eliminate the teasing in the presence of the punisher because the teasing is still being reinforced in multiple ways. It creates some "action" for Junior to relieve his boredom, gives him a sense of control over his sister, and gets lots of attention from Mom and Dad. The cost of the punishment pales when pitted against the existence of these powerful reinforcers. The real solution to the problem lies not in "attacking" the problem behavior with punishment, but in recognizing and managing the reinforcers.

This presents a conundrum to parents. If punishment doesn't work, then how is it possible to discipline a child? Jordan Riak (2002), Director of Parents and Teachers Against Violence in Education (PTAVE), offers a solution in the form of a paradigm shift. Some of his ideas are reflected in this chapter. He believes that the focus of discipline is more aptly directed at the parent instead of the child. It's not something you do to the child, it's a way of showing the child how to be. Discipline starts with the adult's perception of the child's true needs. But a misunderstanding of those needs can leave the door open to counterproductive responses by the parent. In reality, most parents simply react to the child in a manner consistent with what they witnessed and experienced at the hands of their parents while growing up. And now, as adults in charge of their own children, they mindlessly discipline as they were disciplined. Unless parents make a conscious effort to change this automatic intergenerational discipline pattern, it will be passed on to their children.

Too often discipline consists of getting angry and punishing the child with a spanking, yelling, or grounding. In other words, to punish means to vent anger at the child. Anger is the primary motivator. But with this approach, one is already headed down the wrong path.

Some spanking advocates advise that one should never

spank when angry. This is a tacit acknowledgment that spanking often is a result of parents' anger—that it is easy to overreact, hit too hard, and injure a child. The fatal flaw in this advice is that research clearly indicates punishment has no impact on behavior if it is not administered immediately (Camp, Raymond, & Church, 1967). Therefore, if an angry parent waits until he has cooled off before punishing, the whole purpose of punishment has been defeated. There are other spanking advocates who apparently are willing to ignore the obvious physical dangers associated with overreaction. They advise parents to respond without delay to a child's misbehavior. Upon examination of both options: a) to punish spontaneously, with all its risks and meager temporary benefits or b) to wait until one has cooled down before punishing and accrue even fewer benefits, it should become obvious that neither choice is a good one. It makes far better sense for parents to learn and employ non-spanking methods. They have been proven to work, and are without the high risk of negative side effects.

Riak says that discipline must begin with the parent. Parents must first learn to manage their own emotions in a disciplined manner by thinking, "How do I stand back and rationally assess the problem, think of possible solutions, and move to the next step without succumbing to the natural impulse to strike out in anger. Discipline begins with me. I need to act with self-control." Attempting to guide a child without learning alternatives to those reactions copied blindly from one's own childhood, is destined to fail.

Raising a child is the most difficult and demanding task any of us will ever undertake. To do so without self-discipline, self-understanding, and knowledge of child development, but by merely relying on old habits and impulses, is like jumping out of an airplane and saying ,"I'll figure out how to work the parachute on my way down." At that point it's too late to do it correctly. Granted, behavior is complex and today's families are under enormous stress. No one can be expected to parent correctly all of the time. And a simple, all-purpose, fool-proof recipe book on how to be a perfect parent hasn't been written, and probably will never be written. What is most important is to set a family tone of love, caring, and mutual respect. A positive tone sets the stage for easier and more successful family interactions. If parents make an occasional slip, reverting to their old impulse-driven habits, it's not the end of the world. A positive family climate works as a powerful antidote to the occasional mistake.

Parents foolishly will punish a child at a restaurant dinner table for an infraction like throwing crayons all over the table and pouting instead of picking them up. They may say something like, "You naughty girl! Do you want a spanking? There's no dessert for you, young lady, if you're going to behave like this." The situation is instantly turned into a very bad experience filled with negative messages, bad feelings, and is almost certainly headed for a crash landing. It is all so unnecessary! If, instead, the parent starts from a position of self-discipline, she may realize that her five-year-old is tired, stressed, and at the end of her rope after a long, hard day. She cannot handle the frustration of sitting still and obeying all the expected social rules. The wise parent recognizes the source of the child's apparent misbehavior. Perhaps the mother is embarrassed by having others see her child's breach of good conduct, but she should put such considerations aside. After all, this is not a scene from a Shirley Temple movie. This is real life. The mother must keep focused on the true needs of her child, not the impression she is making on strangers. She might handle the situation this way: "Sierra, the pizza is coming soon. But where will the waitress put it if the crayons are all over the table? Here, I'll pick up this one and you can help me get the others. Here's the green one. Can you get the yellow one? Thank you. Now, where's the blue one? Sierra! You know all the colors. Did you learn that at school?" The mother skillfully redirects the child onto safe territory. Now Sierra is engaged in an activity she understands, has control of, and, as a bonus, has proudly displayed her mastery of colors.

Five-year-olds are naturally industrious. Tapping into this strength is a smart move. It's better for Sierra to feel good about helping mom and getting a word of praise about her accomplishments, than to have her frustrations compounded by a disapproving, threatening, and angry parent. Can't you just see a five-year-old smiling and beaming with pride in this scenario? She's really learned a lot of positive lessons about proper behavior, patience, self-control, respect for the dignity of others, creative solutions, and family bonding. This is what healthy discipline is all about!

Remember, positive reinforcement is the most powerful kid motivator in the world. In other words, everyone can learn to manage children's behavior without hitting, yelling, being angry, and asserting power. It is not necessary to conclude, "If I am not allowed to hit my kid, then I don't know what to do. I won't be able to discipline him at all anymore." This attitude is child abuse in disguise. The child's discipline is being neglected due to the lack of effort put forth by the parent to sort out what is happening and teach proper behavior. It takes more time and effort to discipline creatively than to react punitively, but as Murray Straus always says, "Take the time. It's worth it."

Without the motivation to learn and improve, the pattern of impulse-hitting will be transmitted to the next generation. Riak points out that the burden of discipline should not be borne by the child, but by the parent. How well the parent keeps at bay habitual punitive impulses, and supplants them with thoughtful management, makes all the difference.

Some parents attempt to justify punitive control of children with such argument as: "If I don't threaten or punish Johnny, he won't listen. But a swift swat on the bottom or the threat of a grounding gets his attention fast." What those parents fail to understand is that children learn to listen the same way they learn everything else—by imitation. The parent who wants a child to listen, must first model that behavior. The best way a parent can show the child how to be a listener is by listening to the child. While talking to children is a thousandfold better than hitting them, learning to balance talking with listening takes the process of good parenting one vital step further. The child who is listened to is the child who learns to listen. In child rearing, as in all other human relationships, one usually gets what one gives.

Consider this analogy: The prohibition of wife-beating created a social revolution. A wife was no longer considered a husband's property to do with as he pleased. He was no longer allowed to control her by imposing his will through intimidation and physical punishment. However, the new laws did not immediately change men's attitudes. They addressed behavior. Husbands had to refrain from hitting their wives out of fear of becoming social pariahs or having to defend their behavior in a courtroom. The law set in motion a gradual shift in cultural norms that required generations to change the old thought patterns and ways.

Today, boys who rarely or never witness their mother being abused by their father, are highly unlikely to become abusive husbands. Girls who rarely or never see their mothers mistreated by their dads, are highly unlikely to become victimized wives. We no longer accept a husband's right to "lovingly chastise an errant wife." The concept of wife-as-property and husband-as-master, which was once central to family dynamics, has lost its legitimacy. With the advantage of hindsight, we see the terrible price paid by past generations that were trapped in such a belief system. No reasonable person wants to return to the old way. Now we are on the cusp of the next social revolution. It is only a matter of time before the antiquated norms that permit violence to be committed on children in the name of discipline follow suit and join wife beating in the dustbin of atavistic values.

Chapter 7

The Future of Childhood Discipline in America

Over forty years ago Sears, Maccoby, and Levin (1957) were the first to widely report that the use of physical punishment on children by parents was associated with aggression and the weak development of a conscience in their children. A quarter century ago Gil (1974) sounded a call to arms for the abolition of the corporal punishment of children in the U.S.

> Since culturally determined [positive] attitudes toward the use of physical force in child rearing seem to constitute the common core of all physical abuse of children in American society, systematic educational efforts aimed at gradually changing this aspect of child-rearing philosophy and developing clear cut cultural prohibitions and legal sanctions against the use of physical force in rearing children are likely to produce over time the strongest possible reduction of the incidence of physical abuse of children (p. 167).

Since then, hundreds of additional studies have supported and extended their findings. A recent meta-analysis of eighty-eight studies found that the corporal punishment of children is associated with the increase of eleven problem behaviors including aggression, lack of empathy, and mental health problems (Thompson, 1999). When are we, as a society, going to heed these warnings and abolish the use of corporal punishment on our children?

Institutions have already made the switch. All over America

they are adopting the superior behavior-technology method of behavior management—which emphasizes the use of positive reinforcement and response cost—to discipline children. Schools are in the middle of making the transition to nonphysical discipline. Twenty-seven states have abandoned the use of corporal punishment to discipline students in school, while twenty-three states legally permit its use. The twenty-three states that still legally permit its use are: Alabama, Arizona, Arkansas, Colorado, Delaware, Florida, Georgia, Idaho, Indiana, Kansas, Kentucky, Louisiana, Mississippi, Missouri, New Mexico, North Carolina, Ohio, Oklahoma, Pennsylvania, South Carolina, Tennessee, Texas, and Wyoming (see Fig. 2). These are mostly politically conservative states. The number of times children were hit by "educators" in the schools in these states annually now is about half a million. The good news is that most states no longer permit corporal punishment to be used on students. It should not be long before the rest follow suit. Only the political pressure of uninformed parents, administrators, and legislators prevent the remaining states from banning corporal punishment in schools. For those who want to help speed up the inevitable and lobby against the continued use of corporal punishment in these states, the addresses of their chief education officers are listed on the website nospank.net.

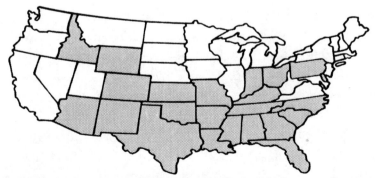

Figure 2. The states that are shaded still permit the use of corporal punishment in schools.

Parents will be the last ones to abandon physical punishment because most of them are not aware of the current research findings. Parenting classes are not required in school, and parents are not required to demonstrate parenting competence through any type of formalized procedure. Manicurists are not allowed to practice without a license. Apparently the public's fingernails are more important to legislators than the well-being of children. Parents can only learn about developmental research findings by seeking out information on their own. Thanks to the American ethic of fierce individualism, the autonomous family tradition, and the attitude that children are the private property of their parents, and therefore have virtually none of the same rights afforded adults, there is a cultural disincentive to do this. I fear that the cultural inertia that favors the use of physical punishment as a means of controlling children's behavior will take generations to turn around. Tens of millions of otherwise happy and exuberant children will be condemned to live a diminished life, a life of anxiety, suffering, or confusion, all because knowledge of the most effective means of discipline and behavior control was not made known to their parents.

There is an ongoing—and what some would consider a raging—debate between pro- and anti-spanking advocates. In reading through the rather extensive literature of spanking apologists, I notice common tactics (Trumbull & Ravenel, 1996),which I will rebut: First, they feature contrary research findings, those studies that found no ill-effects of spanking, or even positive effects, in a limited context (Larzelere, 1998). They concede that hitting infants and teenagers results in injury and aggression, *but not with two-to six-year-olds.* They admit that using a belt or fist is dangerous and humiliating, *but not an open hand.* They confess that spanking children three times a day is too much, maybe abusive, *but not if a child is spanked less often.* They agree that hitting by an angry, emotional parent can leave lasting emotional wounds, bitterness, and resentment, *but not when the parent hits with the "proper attitude."* If one has to use this many qualifications to support an argument, it begins to lose credibility.

Scientists adhere to a principle that determines which of two or more competing theories are correct. It is called the *Law of Parsimony,* or *Occum's Razor.* In essence, it states that the simplest, or most elegant, theory is best, the one that requires the fewest "ifs," exceptions, qualifications, or other twists of logic to explain empirical observations. Using this principle, based upon all the systematic observations available in corporal punishment studies, one must reach a basic, simple conclusion—*hitting children hurts them.* No other conclusion is reasonable or possible without so many disclaimers as to make it hopelessly worthless under the Law of Parsimony. If it takes that many qualifications to spank "the right way" to avoid harming children, then it is too difficult to ever work properly and must be abandoned as an inferior disciplinary practice. Seventy percent of the population can't even program their VCR to record a TV program "the right way" without screwing it up. How are they possibly going to avoid harming their children by hitting "the right way?"

This reminds me of the early days of computer technology in the 1970s. Computer tasks were so cumbersome and difficult to complete properly, that only the brave tried to tackle their use. Of course, there were always the technophiles, called "computer nerds," who thrived on knowing how to thread their way through the confusing array of computer language, codes, manuals, and control commands. But the vast majority hated the feelings of vulnerability, frustration, and looking foolish when we invariably flubbed up somewhere along the way. The over-forty crowd may remember that those were the days of punch cards, TECO, and MS-DOS. I don't care how many times I punched those infernal cards, or keyed in the supposed number of spaces and symbols to move the cursor, or tried to remember the proper command sequence, or whether there was supposed to be a period or comma or space or whatever, I could never get it exactly right! My computer task outcomes were consequently very poor. I would repeatedly get my batch of punch cards returned with a printout that said the task failed because the punch cards were not punched correctly. Actually, they even found a way to make failure difficult to understand by stating it in computer jargon and error numbers that I always had to have someone in-the-know translate for me. Plain English, for some reason, was not good enough for computer operators and programmers to use. No matter how hard I tried, I could never get it right.

However, there were always some who would argue that it was a good system, that I was at fault for not doing things right. Some vested interests even fought to keep the status quo, insisting that I had to learn how to do it right; that there was no possibility of using alternative procedures or systems; that I had to stick with this tricky, difficult, and frustrating system, and should not question it or try to find a better way to accomplish my task. "This is the only way," they proclaimed. Who was I to question it? Thank goodness for research, for curiosity, for progress, for creative and forward thinkers. Those who did not fear change, who wanted a better world of technological tools, were on the case. Steven Jobs and Macintosh came to the rescue in 1984. They fought the old school, the vested interests, the diehards, the status quo, and prevailed. They did not believe that the only way to conduct computer tasks was with a cumbersome, error-prone, and atavistic system. I no longer had to remember hundreds of arcane commands and procedures to accomplish simple computer tasks. It was easy, straightforward, and practically error-free. Everything was intuitive. There was just one rule: Do things as easily and naturally as you normally do. It was not necessary to memorize the minutia of every step in order to avoid disaster. If you want to open a file, point to it and click it open. To get rid of a file, throw it in the trash. How perfect! It revolutionized the world. There's no going back. Everyone can successfully operate a computer now and reap the benefits. We have entered a brave new world of technology that now works *for* us instead of frustrating, controlling, and enslaving us to its impossible demands. Now everyone can easily and successfully make computers do work for them, rather than vice versa. As a result, the world economy has entered an unprecedented period of employment, efficiency, productivity, and prosperity. Of course Bill Gates knocked off the idea, and through a heavy-handed business approach and the power of monopoly, made 50 billion dollars, and manipulated 90% of the world of computer users into making do with Windows instead of the superior Mac OS. But that's beside the point. The world is not always fair. Ninety percent of American parents still spank their children. Oh, and by the way, there is only one simple, elegant, intuitive, and foolproof rule that emerges from the corporal punishment research—*if you don't want to hurt your children, don't hit them.*

In science there are almost always studies that show inconsistent or contradictory results, especially in the behavioral sciences. It is due to the nature of the variable studied, human behavior. It is incredibly complex and difficult to pin down. Just to give you an idea of the enormity of this task, the study of human behavior is the most difficult science known. The sciences that study other natural phenomena such as physics, geology, and chemistry are mere child's play by comparison. They can easily organize their data into laws due to the degree of consistency that exist in their findings. Psychology has to settle for probabilistic outcomes, rather than the certainty of laws. That is why the branch of mathematics used in the social and behavioral sciences is statistics, which is based upon probability. If a child suffers at the hands of abuse or corporal punishment, we can only say that there is an increased chance of being depressed, having Posttraumatic Stress Disorder, Borderline or Antisocial Personality Disorder, an anxiety disorder, or a multitude of other possible deleterious outcomes in adulthood. Unless, of course, the child is "resilient," in which case, he or she, as happened with David Pelzer (who wrote a book in 1995 titled *A Child Called It* about suffering through one of the worse cases of childhood abuse in California history), will go on to become a successful achiever. Any given human behavior is buried and mired in perhaps thousands of confounding variables, called "noise." It is the equivalent to trying to pick out one faint signal of intelligent life in the vast array of radio signals constantly bombarding the earth from outer space, as currently attempted in the SETI project (Search for Extra-Terrestrial Intelligence). They have a supercomputer that monitors thousands of simultaneous radio signals at once and searches for language-like patterns in each one. Picking out a behavioral effect that results from spanking, with any degree of exactness or certainty, when a child is exposed to perhaps millions of other influences, is not easy. Therefore, attempts to do so, while quite noble, are bound to be very error-prone. Where there is error, there are contradictory findings. That does not mean conclusions are premature. As in SETI, if there is one "hit," that is a signal the computer says may be a language from extraterrestrials, it doesn't mean much unless it can be verified with many similar follow-up signals. So far, these "hits" have never been verified with consistent similar follow-up signals. They turned out to be just isolated noise. That is not the case with this corporal-punishment research. There is more than just one "hit," or a study showing deleterious effects of using corporal punishment. The first hit, a study indicating deleterious effects of corporal punishment was followed up by another and another and another. Now there is enough research evidence to show a clear pattern. Scientists start to feel comfortable with a finding when it has been replicated and reproduced in study after study. That is what has happened with this body of research: It has reached enough of a critical mass that the findings are almost impossible to ignore. There are dozens upon dozens of research studies that show the negative impact that corporal punishment has on behavior. All these hits make the noise more readily apparent. For instance, Baumrind's (2001) recent study was the only one of seven longitudinal studies conducted since 1997 that found no significant harmful effects from spanking. With a comparison group of only three subjects, she virtually guaranteed that no harmful side effects of spanking would appear statistically. Some are calling her results the *Baumrind Fallacy* because it stands so isolated in contrast to the large tide of corporal punishment negative effects found by other researchers. For an indication of the extent of this body of research, just turn to the references section at the end of this book and count the number of pages of research cited to support my main thesis, that spanking children leads to undesirable behavioral outcomes. I predict that it is only a matter of time before the literature will so overwhelmingly indicate the need to abandon corporal punishment as ineffective and harmful, that even the most ardent skeptics will have to make concessions as to the validity of the findings. This has already begun to happen. Gershoff (2002), in a five-year meta-analysis research project of 88 corporal punishment studies, has concluded they show a very consistent pattern of 10 negative outcomes in children's emotions and behavior associated with parental use of corporal punishment.

From a public policy standpoint, the future looks promising. I predict it is inevitable that the corporal punishment of children will eventually be banned in the U.S. sometime in the not-too-distant future, and all other countries of the world by the end of this century. How do I know this? There are four main indicators: First, the historical record is on the side of banning corporal punishment. We have a history of banning all inhumane practices, including corporal punishment. Inhumane practices that have been banned throughout history are slavery, torture, and child labor. The use of corporal punishment throughout society has been increasingly abolished, ranging from disallowing its use on wives to soldiers, and prisoners. There is a clear historical trend for extending the reach of the corporal punishment ban to more and more groups. Some animal protection organizations have even gone as far as advocating the protection of animals from physical pain in medical experiments; therefore, it is only a matter of time until we, as a society, become sensitized to the suffering of children in this regard and eventually afford them the same protection virtually every other living group has achieved.

Secondly, as attitudes change, behavior follows. There is a clear trend in the U.S. that attitudes toward the use of corporal punishment on children is softening. The percentage of mothers who agree with the statement, "It is sometimes necessary to discipline a child with a good hard spanking" has decreased steadily from 95% in 1968 to 60% as of 1994 (Straus, 2002). If we project this trend into the future, the rate of rejecting child corporal punishment will probably reach a political critical mass within twenty-five years and then its use will be banned in the U.S. Incidentally, we see a concomitant drop in child abuse in the statistics that corresponds to the attitude change about corporal punishment (Straus & Gelles, 1986). The prevalence of reported abuse of children by their parents on the Conflict Tactics Scale has decreased from 16% of parents abusing their children in 1975 to 10% in 1992 (Straus & Kantor, 1995).

Thirdly, there is a major shift in attitudes toward what types of corporal punishment are now considered appropriate. The shift is from the use of severe forms of corporal punishment on children to milder forms. In the past, using a belt or face-slapping was considered fully acceptable. Now, even ardent adherents of corporal punishment would agree that anything other than the use of an open hand on the bottom is not reasonable physical punishment. The bar of unreasonable forms of corporal punishment has been considerably raised. If it continues to rise at the rate of the last twenty-five years, all forms of child corporal punishment will seem unreasonable in the not-too-distant future.

Lastly, we see a trend to abolish the corporal punishment of children by country. So far, Sweden in 1979, Finland in 1984, Norway in 1987, Austria in 1989, Cyprus in 1994, Latvia in 1998, Croatia in 1999, with Italy, Israel, and Denmark effectively having done so recently. Germany, Switzerland, Poland, Spain, Canada, New Zealand, Mexico, Namibia, South Africa, Sri Lanka, Jamaica, the Republic of Ireland, Belgium, Korea, and the United Kingdom are currently engaged in legal or educational campaigns to ban the corporal punishment of children (EPOCH-USA, 1999). Typically, there is a domino effect that occurs with progressive attitudes wherein change travels from the most socially progressive countries to other countries similar in culture and socioeconomic status. This European social trend will undoubtedly leap the Atlantic and eventually make its way to the United States or Canada in the not-too-distant future. When hitting children finally does become illegal in America, there will be a more rapid decline in the attitude of acceptance toward corporal punishment, and a new cultural norm will emerge that disavows the striking of children by their parents.

The country of Sweden offers a living laboratory of what happens to a society that bans the use of corporal punishment in the home. Although corporal punishment had been banned in Sweden's schools since 1958, child abuse was still prevalent in the 1970s. Policy makers reasoned that child abuse begins with the right of parents to hit their children and therefore the process might be short-circuited by preventing this first step of child abuse from occurring. They passed a national law in 1979 that banned the use of physical punishment on children in the home or other forms of humiliating treatment. It states, "children are entitled to care, security, and a good upbringing.

Children are to be treated with respect for their person and individuality, and may not be subjected to physical punishment or other injurious or humiliating treatment" (Chapter 6, Section 1, Foraldrabalken). The law was made more palatable to constituents by including no penalties for noncompliance. Even though there are no teeth in this law, it does have value, particularly in the area of raising consciousness levels on the issue. Since it became clear to children that hitting them was unacceptable, they have been more likely to report cases of substantiated child abuse. This facilitates earlier and more effective child abuse interventions by social service agencies. The Swedish government has coupled the law with a comprehensive parent education campaign—the most extensive public education campaign ever in Sweden (Durrant, 1994). A booklet entitled *Can You Bring up Children Successfully Without Smacking and Spanking?* was mailed to every household with children in the country. It conveyed the message that spanking can cause physical and psychological harm, it proposed alternative types of discipline, and provided a list of help sources. It made parents think twice before striking their children. Parents were provided with additional education in child health service locations. The media also gave the law wide coverage. The school curriculum in grades seven through nine incorporated the law's message into parenting and child development classes. All of this has had the effect of making it easier for Swedish parents to stop physical punishment than to try to defend its continued use.

What effect did this law, and all the related parenting education, have a decade later? Dr. Adrienne Haeuser, a professor at the University of Wisconsin/Milwaukee and Project Director for the National Committee for the Prevention of Child Abuse, provides one answer: She traveled to Sweden in 1988 to conduct research on the pioneering law under a grant from the National Center of Child Abuse and Neglect. She administered a structured interview to sixteen national authorities, forty-six human services professionals, sixteen native Swedish parents, and numerous other parents (Haeuser, 1990). She found that "None of the parents I met on my trip had to 'think twice' about hitting their children. As beneficiaries of the school program and the government's public education materials, they had internalized the message. Both parents and professionals agreed that the generational transmission of hitting children as a means of childrearing has been broken."

Durrant (2000) used public crime data to answer the question, is "legal sanctioning of corporal punishment necessary to socialize children and youth effectively?" Contrary to the "Chicken Little's" warning that children will be uncontrollable and lack discipline without the threat of corporal punishment, virtually all types of crime have diminished in Sweden since the ban was passed. The majority of Swedish adolescents who grew up during the ban report having never been struck by their parents with the remaining saying that they have only been hit once or twice in their lives. Did the lack of physical punishment make them unruly? No, just the opposite occurred. Durrant found declining adolescent rates of theft, narcotics trafficking, rape, and alcohol and drug use. Apparently Swedish youth are functioning more adaptively now than they did before the ban. Swedish parents now rely on verbal conflict resolution skills rather than letting the switch do the talking for them. Susan Bitensky (1996), Professor of Law at Detroit College of Law at Michigan State University, wrote an article examining some of the legal issues involved in prohibiting the use of corporal punishment on children.

If your adult neighbor engaged in offensive or irritating behavior, would you hit him? Probably not. What if that neighbor had less-than-average adult physical or mental abilities? Given his relative vulnerability, you would probably be even less likely to "knock" some sense into him. And, if you loved that neighbor as if he were a family member, hitting him would seem a downright repellent way of dealing with the situation. Now imagine that the offender is your child—typically, a person of less-than-average adult abilities and a person you love as a family member. Would you hit him? Many parents would do so, not out of meanness, but out of the conviction that loving child rearing requires no less.

It is assumed in our society that parents should be able to spank or otherwise corporally punish their children as a corrective or educational measure, i.e., as a means of teaching children how to behave. This assumption is so ingrained and longstanding that it is almost never questioned. Its vitality owes much to the role of law: on the one hand, parents have a federal constitutional right to rear their children in accordance with their own beliefs; on the other hand, there is no legal prohibition in the United States against parents spanking their children. In fact, state laws generally permit parents to use "reasonable" corporal punishment on their offspring. Nevertheless, some would have the law play an even stronger rule in this regard. A bill is pending in Congress—the Parental Rights and Responsibilities Act—which expressly provides for a federal parental right to use "reasonable corporal discipline" in raising children. In addition, over the last two years a movement has been underway to convince states to add a Parental Rights Amendment to their constitutions. The proposed amendment declares that the right of parents to direct the upbringing of their children must not be infringed. While it does not deal directly with corporal punishment, the amendment would further support the assumption that the parental right to spank as a means of upbringing is sacrosanct.

If all of our assumptions were always valid, we would need neither to think nor to change. We could just follow the practices of our forebears. History has shown, however, that assumptions, no matter how old or widespread, can be woefully wrongheaded. At one time slavery was assumed to be legitimate, and physical chastisement of wives was assumed to be every husband's prerogative. We as a society thought through these assumptions and ultimately repudiated them. Perhaps now the time has come to think anew about the assumption that parents should have the right to hit their children. It might turn out to be a well-founded assumption; it also might not.

Our consideration should, of course, be as informed as possible. We should look to psychologists, pediatricians, teachers, and other experts on child development. We should also not be afraid to take a look, for informational purposes, at how people in other countries have responded to this issue. Like us, most of the world does allow parents to administer corporal punishment to their children. But it is a little publicized fact that some of the world does not allow such punishment. Sweden has had a statute on the books since 1979 banning parental corporal punishment of children. In recent years, Norway, Finland, Austria, Denmark and Cyprus have enacted similar statutes. Now Italy has joined the club. On May 1,. Italy's highest court issued a decision prohibiting parental use of corporal punishment on children.

Judge Francesco Ippolito, who wrote the opinion for the Italian Supreme Court of Cassation, has been willing to share his insights into the court's intentions and meaning beyond the reported decision. In an interview with me in Rome, Ippolito explained that he was speaking out because the judges regard the message in their decision as extremely important to children's well-being.

The case arose when Natalino Cambria took to repeatedly subjecting his ten-year-old daughter to heavy beatings, purportedly to correct her behavior. He would hit or kick the girl for lying, for getting bad grades or for almost any failure to live up to her father's standards. Cambria was prosecuted and convicted of mistreatment. On appeal to the Italian Supreme Court the father argued, among other things, that he should not have been convicted because he had lacked the requisite intent to mistreat a child; he contended that his intent in beating Danila had been merely to correct her wayward behavior. The court rejected this defense and ruled that Cambria had violated the statutory provision making mistreatment of children a crime.

The Cambria case involved the systematic use of serious violence against a child. However, the court's ruling was by no means confined to those facts. According to Ippolito, the court considered the case as an opportunity to establish the legal principle that parents in Italy are absolutely forbidden from using any violence or corporal punishment to correct their children's conduct. That is why, in addition to upholding Cambria's conviction for mistreatment, the court declared without the least equivocation that "the use of violence for educational purposes can no longer be considered lawful."

What considerations prompted the court to take this dramatic step? Judge Ippolito explained that the court drew upon the ideas and values of modern Italian society—Italian family values, if you will—as reflected in current Italian law. The court emphasized three values in particular: First, the Italian Constitution and family laws express an overriding concern with the dignity of the individual. These laws conceive that minors are entitled to be treated with a dignity equal to that accorded adults. Second, the Italian Constitution manifests a societal repudiation of violence as a way of resolving problems, either amongst nations or individuals. Third, Italy as a party to the UN Convention on the Rights of the Child has embraced that treaty's tenets that children have a right to the harmonious development of their personality and that children should be raised in the spirit of peace and tolerance. The Supreme Court reasoned that parental use of violence in the name of child rearing would be inconsistent with each of these values. Indeed, Judge Ippolito stressed that the new legal principle is directed at undoing the very "basis of the whole problem of violence against children."

It is true that many of our laws are different than Italian laws. Not all American family values are or should be the same as Italian family values. But surely we share with Italian parents love for our children and a desire for their healthy development. Surely, as civilized human beings, we share a regard for human dignity and a repugnance to violence. This common ground is reason enough to make us more circumspect about the assumption that parents should have the right to spank their children for educational purposes.

It may turn out that the Italians are on to something—that there are better ways of disciplining and guiding our children. Upon further reflection, we may find that the age-old admonition to "do unto others as you would have them do unto you" should apply to doing unto our children as well as unto our neighbors.

Even dogs have advocates that are demanding better treatment than our children are getting. Contemporary dog trainers are vehemently against hitting dogs to train them (DeRosa, 1993). "We don't know of any dog training programs today that take a hard-handed approach," reports Suzanne Lustig of the American Kennel Club. One of the new breed of dog trainers that favor the more humane approach, Warren Eckstein, the host of a weekly pet radio show says, "Hitting [dogs] just creates animosity. When you teach good behavior, a lot of bad behavior disappears." Dr. Jim Humphries, a veterinarian, is against the "newspaper on the snout" approach to dog obedience training because, "If you call your dog and he doesn't come and you hit him, then the dog says 'It is not wise to be around this person.' Then they either bite back or they cower and urinate, and create a submissive cycle that never gets corrected." Brian Kilcommons, a dog trainer, and author of *Good Owners, Great Dogs,* is also against hitting dogs to train them "because it wouldn't correct the problem and will put you in a primary-bite situation. Aggression begets aggression. People think that training is something that is unpleasant but it doesn't have to be." And finally, Wayne Cavannaugh, Communications Vice President of the American Kennel Club, concurs, "Dogs are going to want to please you if you treat them nicely. A lot of people get dogs and try the hard-knocks routine and all of a sudden the dog is eighteen months old and is out of control. It's just not the way to train dogs. Reward training . . . reinforces the human-canine bond (DeRosa, 1993, p. D1)." Champion dog owners have already discovered the principles of effective discipline that most social scientists advocate. How long will it take parents to come to the same realization?

Public Policy Implications

The large body of research that finds corporal punishment has numerous and serious behavioral side effects indicates a need to address this practice as a public health issue (Giles-Sims, Straus, & Sugarman, 1995). The high prevalence and rate of spanking in the U.S. is a serious threat to the healthy development of our children. Other public health threats, like smoking and drunk driving, are addressed with public awareness and education campaigns, at a minimum. So far the physical and psychological damage inflicted upon our children by the use of corporal punishment has been totally ignored from a public health policy standpoint.

A rough estimate of the financial burden the belief in using corporal punishment on children places on society should make salient the urgency of initiating an all-out assault against it, akin to the war on poverty. The potential savings is enormous. What would be the total savings possible if the use of corporal punishment on children were eliminated and there were no more deleterious side effects? Sweden provides a living example of how effective the abolition of corporal punishment can be in reducing the incidence of child abuse and injury: Swedish rates of child abuse and family child homicide is only one-half the rate found in the U.S. (Gelles & Edfeldt, 1988). The annual incidence of child maltreatment cases referred to Stockholm hospitals has declined to one-sixth of the 1970 rate (Haeuser, 1990).

Here are some rough estimates of the potential savings: Figure a savings of $250,000 each for the 2,000 children who are killed each year by their parents for ambulance, hospital, funeral, law enforcement, child service workers, prosecution, and incarceration costs (Cavaliere, 1995). That adds up to 500 million dollars. Conservatively there are one million cases of child abuse each year in the U.S. (Sedlak & Broadhurst, 1996). Some sources report the actual number is ten times higher. If it costs $5,000, on the average, for child protective services to deal with each child-abuse case, including the cost of foster care, that comes to 5 billion dollars. The medical cost of treating the 565,000 who are seriously injured each year by parents using corporal punishment would conservatively average $10,000 per child. The total cost would be 5.65 billion dollars. The newspaper article appearing in this book that reports about the Shaken Baby Syndrome case gives an idea of the staggering costs associated with severe injury to a child. Tedi, the baby who suffered from Shaken Baby Syndrome at the hands of her babysitter, spent the first two weeks after the incident in the hospital's ICU at a cost of $198,000. The perpetrator was sentenced to four and a half to twenty years in prison at a cost of $25,000 per year to the taxpayers. The rest of Tedi's life will be filled with wheelchairs, braces, rehabilitation equipment, and operations to resize the plastic plate in her head as she grows, and constant care. Her mother had to quit her job and go on welfare to care for Tedi and cover the costs of her medical needs. How many millions of dollars and countless suffering will this needless tragedy consume just because Tedi's babysitter believed in corporal punishment? And this is the cost of *only one case* of injury due to corporal punishment! If we factor in the costs of mental health treatment and the cost of crime bred by the use of corporal punishment, the cost becomes astronomical.

I believe that we could conservatively reduce mental health problems and crime by twenty-five percent if we eliminated the use of corporal punishment in this country. I say this due to my clinical experience as a psychologist. My practice includes providing psychotherapy to parolees, to help them successfully complete parole and not recidivate, and to Medicaid recipients to help alleviate their mental health problems. The vast majority of these patients were abused in childhood at the hands of their parents in the name of physical discipline. As a result, they suffer from some combination of depression, anxiety, low self-esteem, Posttraumatic Stress Disorder, impulsiveness, addiction, aggressiveness, social anxiety, or lack of conscience. The annual cost of crime in the U.S. totals 1.7 trillion dollars (Anderson, in press), and mental health care costs total 150 billion dollars (Rice & Miller, 1993). One fourth of both comes to 462 billion dollars. Added all together, I estimate the belief that corporal punishment is proper costs the U.S. economy about 470 billion dollars annually. That's a pretty hefty price tag for a mistaken belief! If public policy was decided rationally, rather than politically, we, as a country, would make the abolition of corporal punishment our number one public policy priority.

How could we address corporal punishment in our public policy? We need to include corporal punishment in our public health agenda with an advertising campaign to increase awareness of the problem, such as has been used to increase seat belt use. It should consist of a warning to parents that spanking is never appropriate and that it has serious side effects. Next, we need to educate parents about alternatives to corporal punishment and how to use them. Preliminary research indicates that education can contribute to the cessation of corporal punishment (Davis, 1999). Parenting education classes should be widely available, free, convenient, and their use by everyone highly encouraged. A special effort should be made to target those groups that are least likely to learn about the deleterious effects of spanking and most likely to use it (Dietz, 1997). They include parents with less than a high school education and parents whose income is in the poverty range. In pilot programs, parents have been shown to respond favorably to learning about positive parenting techniques and favoring positive reinforcement and time-out over medication and spanking (Miller & Kelly, 1992). Those professionals who are in a position to come into contact with parents and influence them, such as teachers, counselors, social workers, and physicians, need to be targeted as ambassadors for non-violent parenting techniques. Ultimately, we would need to ban corporal punishment legislatively in order to have a substantial impact on changing attitudes and behaviors, as occurred in Sweden. American parents would be more likely to support a legislative ban on corporal punishment if it could be demonstrated that it would reduce child injuries and child abuse (Deley, 1988; Durrant, 1994) and be provided with assurance that it does not imply or require permissiveness (Deley, 1988).

Chamberlin (1996) argues that addressing single risk factors, such as spanking, is not effective in promoting positive parenting and reducing developmentally poor outcomes. He advocates a multimodal approach to improving parenting practices that implements community-wide primary prevention programs. This approach would include prenatal care, home visitation training in positive parent-child interaction techniques, early childhood enrichment programs, parenting classes, paid pregnancy and child care leave, high-quality affordable child care, and neighborhood family resource centers. This approach makes a noble attempt to raise the quality of development in our nation's children. It is a wonderful idea and, no doubt, will ultimately be implemented, and succeed some day in the distant future, when politicians place a higher priority on children's welfare than the corporate welfare of their main political contributors.

In the meantime, where is a good place to start improving the developmental outcomes of children? It is with a single, relevant, concrete, and highly related issue—spanking. All social movements gain political momentum this way. They begin humbly, with a single concrete issue or event, that the media and public can easily understand and digest. Witness Maureen Kanka and Megan's Law, and Candy Lightner and Mother's Against Drunk Drivers, and Rosa Parks and the Civil Rights Movement. These single issue causes progress developmentally by gradually growing and reverberating throughout a whole political arena. Look at how much political and societal change has occurred in the areas of victim's rights, drinking and driving, and discrimination as a result of the above three single issues. There needs to be a single concrete starting point for all causes. If that point is sufficient to tap into the media's, public's, and politicians' primal concerns, then a bandwagon effect will ensue, leading to substantial societal change. Just as abortion, crime, school prayer, and discrimination are primal issues that have generated the power to mobilize people and resources, so does corporal punishment.

Corporal punishment is not so much a single issue as would appear at first glance. More accurately, it represents more of a syndrome. Those who rely on corporal punishment as a disciplinary tool are more likely to be less knowledgeable about child development, have fewer communication skills, live in a high-stress world of underemployment and poor relationships, come from dysfunctional families, and lack psychological and financial resources. Imagine the reaction of a parent who fits the above description, or any parent who spanks, when told authoritatively, "You should not hit your children when disciplining them," by any or all of the following: a social worker, pediatrician, counselor, politician, behavioral science researcher, respected media outlet, or by the weight of law, as in Sweden. A powerful psychological chain of events would immediately ensue, probably starting off with an acute case of cognitive dissonance that would go something like this:

Parent: "If I can't spank my kids, then how can I discipline them? How else can I keep my child from running out in the street and getting hit by a car?"

Authority: "Spanking doesn't work. It causes more problems than it solves. It only appears to work in the short run. This is an illusion. There is a substantial body of research that shows using it will cause exactly the opposite of what you want to occur in the long run."

Parent: "Like what?"

Authority: "Like the thirteen undesirable side effects of punishment such as . . . "

Parent: "What can I do instead that works?"

Of course, change will not occur this quickly or easily in the minds of parents, but the change process will occur, nevertheless, over time, as it has in Sweden. The long term and widespread improvement in parenting practices and resources will develop in response to the impetus provided by banning or discouraging corporal punishment. Less is more. A single issue that captures the imagination of the public will go further and longer in providing change than more ambitious and comprehensive approaches, due to their cost or political resistance. Comprehensive programs are not as palatable to the status quo as incremental change.

If I'm a parent who is told to do those things that will lead to better developmental outcomes in my children, I'll yawn and say, "Yeah, that's a good idea. I'll enroll in a parenting course someday but for now I'm already getting along okay." But if I'm told, "You can't spank your kids anymore," I will be compelled to take action now. I will need to search for alternatives and resources. This will create a demand for services. In a free enterprise and entrepreneurial culture like ours, the demand will quickly be filled by educational, health, community and private entities. La Leche League would not exist if mothers did not feel the need for a more comprehensive source of information on how to successfully breastfeed their babies than what is provided in hospital maternity wards. Alcoholics Anonymous, the school DARE drug prevention education program, prison drug abuse education, Synanon, adult and adolescent in-patient recovery programs, DUI driving schools, the Drug Enforcement Agency, Hazelden self-help recovery books, and outpatient substance abuse recovery programs were all created in response to a single issue problem—drug abuse.

If I am convinced that it is not a good idea to spank my children and feel the need to stop, what must I do to change? Just as in the case of changing attitudes toward domestic violence, I first have to learn to control the impulse to hit. What services could I seek out? It could be social support resources such as Parents Anonymous or self-help books on anger control and alternative discipline techniques. What about commercial parent training classes such as Parent Effectiveness Training? Advice from the pediatrician? Respite care? I wouldn't seek out or use any of these resources if I was not convinced of the need to stop hitting my children. The single developmental risk factor of spanking acts as the perfect issue upon which to effectively rally for a coalition of all the comprehensive community services sought by those like Robert Chamberlin.

Changing Societal Norms

The use of physical punishment has deep religious and legal cultural roots (Foucault, 1979; Greven, 1990). Common law in every state allows the use of physical punishment. Virtually everyone is familiar with the biblical paraphrase "Spare the rod and spoil the child," actually from a poem by Samuel Butler in 1664 (Religious Tolerance, 1999). In one study, most parents did not strongly disagree with the statement "Parents have a right to slap their teenage children who talk back to them" and most agreed that "spanking children helps them to be better people when they grow up" (Moore & Straus, 1987). This high degree of approval of physical punishment is unfortunate because those parents who overtly approve of it strike their children more often, up to 4.9 times more than parents who disapprove (Straus, 1991). Murray Straus (1991) believes the cultural norm of physical punishment is implicitly perpetuated in the family from parents to children through the parents' strong approval and use of it on their children. The pressure that this cultural norm exerts on parents to hit their children is even more insidious given that there is recent evidence that many parents do not even believe that hitting kids is effective as a discipline technique, *but do it anyway* (Dietz, 1997). The 1979 Swedish law banning the corporal punishment of children does not provide for any penalties against convicted parents. Its main purpose was to establish a norm against all types of physical punishment of children (Deley, 1988).

What will it take to break through this cultural norm that manifests itself in a perpetuating cycle of family violence? The religious aspect must first be addressed. Some corporal punishment apologists point to the Bible to defend the use of physical punishment on children. They believe the Book of Proverbs commands its use. Some religious conservatives are associated with the support of corporal punishment on children (Ellison, 1996; Grasmich, Bursik, & Kimpel, 1991). There are three main arguments against this religious tenet (Maurer & Wallerstein, 1985):

This first is that nowhere in the Bible is there any endorsement of striking children on their buttocks. A careful reading of the Bible reveals that, in fact, it does not say "Spare the rod and spoil the child." It actually says "He that spareth the rod hateth his son, but he who loveth him chastiseth him betimes" (Proverbs 13:24).

The second argument about Proverbs 13:24 is that there is another way to interpret this verse based upon what is meant by the use of the term rod. Does it mean a spanking stick like a switch or does rod symbolize something else? The rod is many things in the Bible. It symbolizes miraculous power, as when Moses used it to part the waters of the Red Sea (Exodus 14:16). The rod also symbolized wisdom (Proverbs 29:15). Levi's rod blossomed into a plant (Numbers 17:8). The rod was sometimes a symbol of God's anger (Psalms 89:32), but it also symbolized His gentle guidance as in "Thy rod and staff, they comfort me" (Psalms 23:4). How can we be sure which meaning of the word rod is contained in Proverbs 13:24? Some Bible adherents now interpret the word rod to imply guidance rather than corporal punishment since the shepherd's rod was his staff, which he used to guide rather than beat his sheep (Huber, 1981).

The third argument relates to selective perception. If an alcoholic was intent upon rationalizing his consumption of alcohol, he could point to Proverbs 31:6-7 to do so, "Give strong drink unto him that is ready to perish, and wine unto those that be of heavy hearts. Let him drink, and forget his poverty, and remember his misery no more." If one insists upon obeying the corporal punishment interpretation of Proverbs 13:24, then one should, in order to be consistent, obey all the other Bible verses related to the use of corporal punishment. If a person consistently supported the other related verses, he would then allow corporal punishment to be used on anyone. Remember Shakespeare's immortal words, "The devil can cite Scripture for his purpose."

Studying the Bible as a whole clearly shows that God does not approve of everything said or done in the Bible because the Bible presents the history of sinful men and the consequences of their actions. A good interpretation of scripture relies upon spiritual discernment. A passage must be considered in context and in relation to the spirit of the Bible as a whole. In the New Testament, God has given the final revelation of Himself in the message and work of Jesus Christ, who clarified the Old Testament (Hebrews 1:1-5). Parents who look to the Bible to guide their parenting could choose to follow many New Testament verses, among which are; "Fathers, provoke not your children to anger, lest they be discouraged" (Colossians 3:21); "And be ye kind one to another, tenderhearted, forgiving one another, even as God for Christ's sake hath forgiven you" (Ephesians 4:32).

I like to think of the rod as giving guidance as well as giving wisdom; "The rod and reproof gives wisdom" (Proverbs 29:15), which brings us back to the Latin meaning of the word discipline, *disciplina*, translated as "to teach." "Spare the rod . . . " is a call to teach, not punish. Proverbs 22:15 declares, "Foolishness is bound in the heart of a child, but the rod of correction will drive it far from him." We can correct children's foolish behavior by teaching them how to engage in wiser behavior. The most effective way to accomplish this is to provide direction for our children so they can learn. It won't happen by hitting them. Hitting them will only cause them to behave aggressively and fear adults. Providing children an acceptable sense of direction occurs through the use of the alternatives to corporal punishment. The apostle John wrote in I John 4:16-18, "There is no fear in love; but perfect love casteth out fear: because fear is torment. He that fearest is not made perfect in love."

I am convinced that, deep down, parents never really feel good about hitting their children. They suspect that at some level it is the wrong thing to do. The main reason they hit them is because they don't know what else to do. I believe very strongly that if they really knew how well the alternatives worked they would totally abandon corporal punishment forever.

Albert Bandura proposes a society-wide alternative to punishment for all types of infractions in every area of society: He instead calls for restitutive sanctions for children, students, and lawbreakers. Whatever damages are assessed against transgressors, they would then be "sentenced" to repayment. For instance, a child caught stealing from a store would be required to repay the store for what he took rather than be spanked. This avoids the problems associated with punitive sanctions such as corporal punishment by parents, educators, and imprisonment for nonviolent offenders (Bandura, 1986).

What would life in America be like without corporal punishment? According to Murray Straus (1994) we would have a more humane society, where loving parents would not be expected to hurt their children. When parents adopt non-violent ways of disciplining their children, the level of violence, crime, depression, masochistic sex, child abuse, divorce, and stress will be reduced in our society. Parenting will be easier and more pleasurable. Families will be happier. Children will be better behaved. Spousal abuse will be less frequent. There will be a closer bond between parents and children. The economy will benefit from spending less money to control and treat crime and mental disorders. Humanity will benefit from profound and far-reaching benefits. In other words, we will be a less violent, healthier, and wealthier society.

So what about the future of discipline in America? Well, as a great advocate of nonviolent change in America once said, "I have a dream." My dream is that someday soon we will care enough about our children to be as humane in their treatment as contemporary dog trainers are with their animals. Someday we will look back on the use of corporal punishment with the same horror that we now look back upon the use of forced child labor during the early days of the industrial revolution and the right of husbands to "physically chastise an errant wife" a century ago. When that day comes, people who read about corporal punishment in their history books will exclaim, "How could they be so barbaric back then, the way they hit children routinely. Why didn't they protect them with laws against being struck by others, like they did with adults? Didn't they care? Didn't they think children were important?"

I challenge all those who read this book, and lawmakers throughout America, to do everything you can to give our children a present worthy of the new millennium—freedom from cruel and unusual punishment.

Chapter 8

Resources
Organizations Committed to Ending Corporal Punishment

Due, in part, to the overwhelming evidence of the damaging effects of corporal punishment, numerous organizations, from all over the world, are dedicated to its abolishment. Following is a list of these organizations found on the web site nospank.net.

1. Ending Physical Punishment of Children Worldwide (EPOCH).
    77 Holloway Road, London N7 8JZ Phone: 0171 700 0627; Fax: 0171 700 1105;
    E-mail: epoch-worldwide@mcr1.poptel.org.uk
    This is a worldwide federation that works toward the abolishment of corporal punishment through the use of education and legal reform.

2. Center for Effective Discipline, EPOCH-USA, National Coalition to Abolish Corporal Punishment in Schools (NCACPS)
    155 W. Main Street, Suite #1603, Columbus, OH 43215
    Phone: (614) 221-8829
    Fax: (614) 221-2110; URL: www.stophitting.com

    The Center for Effective Discipline provides educational material to the public about corporal punishment and the use of alternatives. They advocate to end the use of parental corporal punishment. Sample statements and resolutions to propose antispanking legislation are available. EPOCH-USA is the American component of EPOCH-Worldwide. NCACPS is a coalition that provides information to the public and media on the progress of banning corporal punishment.

Proclamation Opposing Corporal Punishment of Children:

WHEREAS, *all children need guidance and deserve to grow up in an environment free from physical harm and*

WHEREAS, *millions of children suffer child abuse each year in the name of discipline, and*

WHEREAS, *corporal punishment of children provides a poor model for solving interpersonal problems, leads to a pro-violence attitude, and contributes to the cycle of abuse, and*

WHEREAS, *violence to children is a preventable harm, and*

WHEREAS, *preventing physical violence to children includes learning and using non-violent discipline methods,*

NOW, THEREFORE, *EPOCH-USA will seek to end corporal punishment of children by all persons, including parents, through education and legal reform. EPOCH-USA advocates child-rearing practices that develop caring, responsible, and self-disciplined adults.*

May 18, 1996
EPOCH-USA Advisory Board Meeting
Washington, D.C.

3. The International Society for the Prevention of Child Abuse and Neglect (ISPCAN)
   200 N. Michigan Ave., Suite 500, Chicago, IL 60601 Phone: (312) 578-1401
   Fax: (312) 578-1405; URL: child-abuse.com/ispcan/; e-mail: kimsispcan@aol.com
   ISPCAN supports any international efforts to protect children.

4. Prevent Child Abuse America
   200 S. Michigan Ave., 17th floor Chicago, IL 60604 Phone: (312) 663-3520
   URL: preventchildabuse.org
   This organization works through education and research to prevent child abuse.

5. Parents Anonymous, Inc. National Office, 675 W Foothill Blvd. Suite 220, Claremont, CA 91711. (909) 621-6184. This is a network of local support groups that help parents who seek to avoid the use of physical punishment.
   URL: parentsanonymous.org

Position Statements on Corporal Punishment by Prominent Organizations

1. United Nations Committee on Rights of Child recommends "that corporal punishment be prohibited by law in the family, care and other institutions."

2. American Academy of Child & Adolescent Psychiatry, Corporal Punishment in Schools—Policy Statement.

3. Society for Adolescent Medicine, Corporal Punishment in Schools—Position Paper Corporal Punishment in Schools (RE9207).

4. American Academy of Pediatrics, Committee on School Health—Policy Statement

5. National Association for the Education of Young Children , Position Statement—"Prohibit corporal punishment in schools and all other programs for children."

6. American School Counselor Association, Corporal Punishment: The Position of the ASCA.

7. National Association of School Psychologists—Corporal Punishment Position Statement, Adopted April 18, 1998. Selected excerpts: "Effective discipline is primarily a matter of instruction rather than punishment. Many means of effective and safe discipline are available. Punishment contingencies in general tend to have negative side effects including leading students to be sneaky and lie about their behavior in order to escape punishment. Corporal punishment is a technique that can easily be abused leading to physical injuries. Evidence indicates that corporal punishment negatively affects the social, psychological, and educational development of students and contributes to the cycle of child abuse and pro-violence attitudes of youth."

8. National Council of Teachers of English, Resolution—1986-87 Executive Committee

9. Florida Chapter of the Florida National Organization for Women (NOW)—Corporal Punishment in Schools—Presented as a resolution to the UNITED STATES House Hearing, Committee on Education and Labor, Subcommittee on Select Education, June 18, 1992.

10. American Public Health Association, Policy Resolution on Corporal Punishment, Approved by the Governing Council, November 7, 1979.

11. The National PTA—Corporal Punishment: Myths and Realities,1991

12. American Academy of Pediatrics—Guidance for Effective Discipline (RE9740), Committee on Psychosocial Aspects of Child and Family Health, April 1998

13. Association for Childhood Education International, A Position Paper (Paintal, 1999).

14. American Psychological Association's Council of Representatives passed a resolution in 1985 opposing, "the use of corporal punishment in school, juvenile facilities, child-care nurseries, and all other institutions, public or private, where children are cared for or educated."

15. American Psychological Association Division 37 (Child, Youth, and Family Services) formally opposes the use of corporal punishment in the schools.

16. National Association of Elementary School Principles

Helplines for Parents Who Want to Stop Hitting

1. National Center for the Study of Corporal Punishment and Alternatives
   Irwin Hyman, PhD, Director, Temple University
   (215) 204-6091.

2. Boy's Town counselor, 1-800-448-3000

Model Statute for Banning the Use of Corporal Punishment on Children

Bitensky (1998) has drafted a statute that is modeled after those in use in the European countries that have banned the use of corporal punishment on children. It emphasizes educational interventions versus criminal liability.

Web sites

1. Jordan Riak, Executive Director of Parents and Teachers Against Violence in Education (PTAVE), has an excellent web site (nospank.net) filled with copious information and resources related to corporal punishment. The site contains letters that can be copied and sent to school officials and politicians to lobby for an end to the use of corporal punishment on children by schools and parents. The site lists 107 organizations in the U.S. that are opposed to the use of corporal punishment.

2. Ending Physical Punishment of Children-USA (EPOCH-USA), the American affiliate of EPOCH Worldwide is dedicated to ending the corporal punishment of children with legal reform and education (stophitting.com).

3. Neverhitachild.org, based in Little Rock, Arkansas, lists articles that argue against the use of corporal punishment. NeverHitAChild.ORG, Little Rock, Arkansas, USA

4. Other web sites: ahealthyme.com; iamyourchild.org; npin.org; child-abuse.org; empathicparenting.org; parentsjournal.com; naturalchild.org; members.aol.com/Luv4MyKidz/bookstore.html; sparethechild.com; child-abuse.com; parentsanonymous.org

Reading Resources

De Zulueta, F. (1994). *From Pain to Violence: The Traumatic Roots of Destructiveness.* Northvale, New Jersey: Jason Aronson, Inc.

Greven, P. (1991). *Spare the Child: The Religious Roots of Punishment and the Psychological Impact of Physical Abuse.* New York: Random House.

Hyman, I. A. and Wise, James H. (1979). *Corporal Punishment in American Education: Readings in History, Practice and*

Alternatives. Philadelphia: Temple University Press.

Hyman, I. A. (1990). *Reading, Writing and the Hickory Stick: The Appalling Story of Physical and Psychological Violence in American Schools*. Boston: Lexington Books.

Hyman, I. (1997). *The Case Against Spanking: How to Discipline Your Child Without Hitting*. San Francisco: Jossey Bass Publishers.

Maurer, A. (1981). *Paddles Away: A Psychological Study of Physical Punishment in Schools*. Palo Alto: R&E Research Associates.

Miller, A. (1983). *For Your Own Good: Hidden Cruelty in Child Rearing and the Roots of Violence*. New York: Farrar, Straus and Giroux.

Newell, P. (1989). *Children are People Too: The Case Against Physical Punishment*. London: Bedford Square Press.

Newson, J., & Newson, E. (1989). *The extent of parental physical punishment in the UK*. London: Approach.

Riak, J. *Plain Talk about Spanking*. Booklet available from PTAVE.

Straus, M. A. (1994). *Beating the devil out of them: Corporal punishment in American Families*. New York: Lexington Books.

Straus, M.A. (2000). *Beating the Devil out of Them: Corporal Punishment in American Families and Its Effects on Children, 2nd Edition*. New Brunswick, NJ: Transaction Publishers.

References

Abramson, L. Y., Metalsky, G. I., & Alloy, L. B. (1989). Hopelessness depression: A theory-based subtype. *Psychological Review*, 96, 358-372.

Acker, M. M., & O'Leary, S. G. (1988). Effects of consistent and inconsistent feedback on inappropriate child behavior. *Behavior Therapy*, 19, 619-624.

Ackerman, J. (August 1, 1995). Man gets 4-1/2—20 years in jail for child-shaking injuries. *Pittsburgh Post-Gazette*.

Allen, D. M., & Tarnowski, K. J. (1989). Depressive characteristics of physically abused children. *Journal of Abnormal Child Psychology*, 17, 1-11.

Anderson, D.A. (in press). The aggregate burden of crime. *Journal of Law and Economics*, October, 2002.

Aronson, E., & Carlsmith, J. M. (1963). Effect of severity of threat on the devaluation of forbidden behavior. *Journal of Abnormal and Social Psychology*, 66, 584-588.

Associated Press. (2000, January 5). $8 million offered to inmates in Attica riot. *The Wheeling Intelligencer*.

Axelrod, S., & Apsche, J. (1983). *The effects of punishment on human behavior*. New York: Academic Press.

Azrin, N. H. & Holtz, W. C. (1966). Punishment. In W. K. Honig (Ed.) *Operant behavior: Areas of research and application*. New York: Appleton-Century-Crofts.

Bachar, E. et al. (1997). Physical punishment and signs of mental distress in normal adolescents. *Adolescence*, 32, 945-959.

Bandura, A. (1969). Social learning theory of identificatory processes. In D. A. Goslin (Ed.) *Handbook of socialization theory and research*. Chicago: Rand McNally.

Bandura, A. (1986). *Social foundations of thought and action.* Englewood Cliffs, NJ: Prentice-Hall.

Bandura, A., Ross, D., & Ross, S. A. (1961). Transmission of aggression through imitation of aggressive models. *Journal of Abnormal and Social Psychology, 63,* 575-582.

Baron, P. H. (1974). Self-esteem, ingratiation, and evaluation of unknown others. *Journal of Personality and Social Psychology, 30,* 104-109.

Bateson, G. (1969). Double bind. In G. Bateson *Steps to an ecology of the mind.* New York: Ballantine, 271-278.

Battle, J. (1987). Relationship between self-esteem and depression in children. *Psychological Reports, 60,* 1187-1190.

Baumrind, D. (1971). Current patterns of parental authority. Developmental *Psychological Monographs, 41,* 1-103.

Baumrind, D. (1978). Parental disciplinary patterns and social competence in children. *Youth and Society, 9,* 239-276.

Baumrind, D. (2001). Does causally relevent research support a blanket injunction against disciplinary spanking by parents? Paper presented at the 109th Annual Convention of the American Psychological Association, August 24th.

Beck, J. (July 25, 1987). School paddling: Take it away! *The Chicago Tribune.*

Berger, A. M., Knutson, J. F. Mehm, J. G., & Perkins, K. A. (1988). The self-report of punitive childhood experiences of young adults and adolescents. *Child Abuse and Neglect, 12,* 251-262.

Berkowitz, L. (1989). Frustration-aggression hypothesis: Examination and reformulation. *Psychological Bulletin, 106,* 59-73.

Bettelheim, B. (1987). *A Good Enough Parent: a Book on Child-Rearing.* New York: Knopf.

Bitensky, S. (July 25, 1996). Final straw: To spank or not to spank? *The Chicago Tribune.*

Bitensky, S. H. (1998). Spare the rod, embrace our humanity: Toward a new legal regime prohibiting corporal punishment of children. *University of Michigan Journal of Law Reform, 31*, 354-391.

Bradshaw, J. (1988). *The family.* Deerfield Beach, FL: Health Communications, Inc.

Brehm, J. W. (1972). *Responses to loss of freedom: A theory of psychological reactance.* Morristown: N. J. General Learning Press.

Brezina, T. (1998). Adolescent-to-parent violence as an adaptation to family strain: An empirical examination.

Bryan, J. W., & Freed, F. W. (1982). Corporal punishment: Normative data and sociological and psychological correlates in a community population. *Journal of Youth and Adolescence, 11*, 77-87.

Burns, N. M., & Straus, M. A. (6 Aug. 1987). Cross-national differences in corporal punishment, infant homicide, and socioeconomic factors. *Family Violence Research Program publication*, University of New Hampshire, Durham, NH 03824.

California Medical Association (Oct. 1985). *Health Tips: Corporal Punishment In Our Schools.* California Medical Education and Research Foundation, Index 479.

Camp, D. S., Raymond, G. A., & Church, R. M. (1967). Temporal relationship between response and punishment. *Journal of Experimental Psychology, 74*, 114-123.

Carson, B. A. (1986). Parents who don't spank: Deviation in the legitimization of physical force. Unpublished PhD dissertation, University of New Hampshire.

Cavaliere, F. (1995). Parents killing kids: A nation's shame. *APA Monitor*, Aug., 34.

Chamberlin, R. W. (1996). It takes a whole village: Working with community coalitions to promote positive parenting and strengthening families. *Pediatrics, 98*, 803-808.

Compas, B., Adelman, H., Freundl, P., Nelson, P., & Taylor, L. (1982). Parent and child causal attributions during clinical interviews. *Journal of Abnormal and Child Psychology*, 10, 77-84.

Coopersmith, S. (1967). *The antecedents of self-esteem.* San Francisco, CA: Freeman.

Daley, W. W. (1988). Physical punishment of children: Sweden and the USA *Journal of Comparative Family Studies*, 19, 419-431.

Davis, P. W. (1999). Corporal punishment cessation. *Journal of Interpersonal Violence*, 14, 492-511.

Day, R. D., Peterson, G., & McCracken, C. (1998). Predicting spanking of younger and older children by mothers and fathers. *Journal of Marriage and the Family*, 60, 79-93.

Dear Abby a.k.a. Jeanne Phillips. (July 1993). Child advocate: Hitting teachers wrong lesson. Kansas City, MO: United Press Syndicate.

Dear Abby a.k.a. Jeanne Phillips. (July 31, 1995). Young love can turn defiant if teens not allowed to meet. Kansas City, MO: United Press Syndicate.

Deci, E. (1975). *Intrinsic motivation.* New York: Plenum.

Deley, W. W. (1988). Physical punishment of children: Sweden and the U.S.A. *Journal of Comparative Family Studies*, 19, 419-431.

DeRosa, R. (1993). Dog training methods without bite. *USA Today*, July 29.

Deur, J. L., & Parke, R. D. (1968). Resistance to extinction and continuous punishment in humans as a function of partial reward and partial punishment. *Psychonomic Science*, 13, 91-92.

Dietz, T. L. (1997). Disciplining children: Characteristics associated with the use of corporal punishment and non-violent discipline. Family Research Laboratory, University of New

Hampshire, Durham, NH 03824. Manuscript # CP45.

Dinkmeyer, D. C. & McKay, G. D. (1997). *Systematic Training for Effective Parenting*, American Guidance Service, Inc.

Dishion, T. J., Patterson, G. R., & Reid, J. B. (1988). Parent an peer factors associated with drug sampling in early adolescence: Implications for treatment. in E. R. Rahdert and J. Grabowski (eds.), Adolescent Drug Abuse: Analyses of Treatment Research. Rockville, MD: National Institute of Drug Abuse.

Dribben, M. (January 14, 1999). When discipline silences, forever. *The Philadelphia Inquirer*.

Dunning, D., Meyerowitz, J. A., & Holtzberg, A. D. (1989). Ambiguity and self-evaluation. *Journal of Personality and Social Psychology*.

Durrant, J. E. (1993-94). Sparing the rod: Manitobans' attitudes toward the abolition of physical discipline and implications for policy change. *Canada's Mental Health*, 4, 2-6.

Durrant, J. E. (2000). Trends in youth crime and well-being since the abolition of corporal punishment in Sweden. *Youth and Society*, 31, 437-455.

Eichmann, C. (1966). *The impact of the Gideon decision on crime and sentencing in Florida*. Tallahassee, FL: Division of Corrections Publications.

Eisenman, R., & Sirgo, H. B. (1991). Liberals versus conservatives: Personality, child-rearing attitudes, and birth order/sex differences. *Bulletin of the Psychonomic Society*, 29, 240-242.

Ellison, C. (1996). Conservative Protestantism and the corporal punishment of children: Clarifying the issues. *Journal for the Scientific Study of Religion*, 35, 1-16.

EPOCH-USA. (1999). Legal reforms: Corporal punishment of children in the family as reported by EPOCH-Worldwide.

[Online]. Available: www.stophitting.com INTERNET

Feshbach, N. D. (1980). Physical punishment: The fraternal twin of child abuse. In R. Barnen (Ed.), *Children and violence. Proceedings of the International Symposium on Violence, Stockholm,* 1979. Stockholm, Sweden: Akademi Literatur.

Festinger, L., & Carlsmith, J. M. (1959). Cognitive consequences of forced compliance. *Journal of Abnormal and Social Psychology,* 58, 203-210.

Fisher, A. E. (1955). The effects of differential early treatment on the social and exploratory behaviour of puppies. Doctoral dissertation, Pennsylvania State University.

Floyd, N. M., & Levin, E.. (1987). An expert finds that bullies and their victims are linked in a strange, unconscious courtship. *People* (April 13), 143-146.

Family Development Resources, Inc. (1990). *Shaking, Hitting, Spanking: What to do Instead.* 3160 Pinebrook Road, Park City, Utah 84060.

Fraiberg, S. (1968). *The magic years: Understanding and handling the problems of early childhood.* New York: Charles Scribner's Sons.

Freedman, J. (1965). Long-term behavioral effects of cognitive dissonance. *Journal of Experimental Social Psychology,* 1, 145-155.

Gelles, R. J., & Edfeldt, A. W. (1988). Violence towards children in the United States and Sweden. *Child Abuse and Neglect,* 10, 501-510.

Gershoff, E.T. (2002). Parental corporal punishment and associated child behaviors and experiences: A meta-analytic and theoretical review. *Psychological Bulletin,* 128, 539-579.

Gil, D. G. (1974). A socio-cultural perspective on physical child abuse. In Leavitt, J. E. (Ed.). *The battered child.* USA: General Learning Corporation.

Giles-Sims, J., Straus, M. A., & Sugarman, D. B. (1995). Child, maternal, and family characteristics associated with spanking. *Family Relations*, 4, 170-176.

Ginott, H. (1965). *Between parent and child*. New York: Avon Books.

Goleman, D. (1995). *Emotional intelligence: Why it can matter more than IQ*. New York: Bantam Books.

Gordon, T. (1989). *Discipline That Works: Promoting Self-Discipline in Children,* New York: Plume/Penguin.

Gordon, T. (2000). *Parent effectiveness training: The proven program for raising responsible children.* Crown Publishing, Inc.

Grasmich, H. G., Bursik, R. J., & Kimpel, M. (1991). Protestant fundamentalism and attitude toward corporal punishment. *Violence and Victims*, 6, 283-98.

Graziano, A. M. (1989). The disinhibition hypothesis and the escalation of violence: Learning to be a monster. Paper presented at the conference of Law and the Legitimization of Violence, S.U.N.Y., Buffalo, N.Y.

Graziano, A. M., & Namaste, K. A. (1990). Parental use of physical force in child discipline. *Journal of Interpersonal Violence*, 5, 449-463.

Greven, P. (1990). *Spare the Child: The Religious Roots of Punishment and the Psychological Impact of Physical Abuse*. New York: Alfred A. Knopf, Inc.

Gunnoe, M. I. & Mariner, C. L. (1997). Toward a developmental-contextual model of the effects of parental spanking on children's aggression. *Archives of Pediatric and Adolescent Medicine*, 151, 768-775.

Haeuser, A. A. (1990, September). Banning parental use of physical punishment: Success in Sweden. Paper presented at the Eighth Annual Congress on Child Abuse and Neglect, Hamburg, Germany.

Hardin, G. (1968). The tragedy of the commons. *Science*, 162, 1243-1248.

Hare, R. D. (1970). *Psychopathy*. New York: Wiley.

Harriet, et al. (1999). *Canadian Medical Association Journal*,

Harrington, D. M., Block, J., & Block, J. H. (1987). Testing aspects of Carl Rogers' theory of creative environments: Child rearing antecedents of creative potential in young adolescents. *Journal of Personality and Social Psychology*, 52, 851-856.

Haskett, M. E., & Kistner, J. A. (1991). Social interactions and peer conceptions of young physically abused children. *Child Development*, 62, 979-990.

Heller, J. F., Pallak, M. S., & Picek, J. M. (1973). The interactive effects of intent and threat on boomerang attitude change. *Journal of Personality and Social Psychology*, 26, 273-279.

Hidlay, W. (February 24, 1987). Aggression not linked to success. The Associated Press.

Hilberman, E., & Munson, K. (1977-78). Sixty battered women. *Victimology*: An International Journal, 2, 3-4.

Himelstein, S., Graham, S., Weiner, B. (1991). An attributional analysis of maternal beliefs about the importance of child-rearing practices. *Child Development*, 62, 301-310.

Hoffman, M. L. (1960). Power assertion by the parent and its impact on the child. *Child Development*, 31, 129-143.

Hoffman, H. S., Fleshler, M., & Jensen, P. K. (1963). Stimulus aspects of aversive controls: The retention of conditioned suppression. *Journal of Experiential Analysis of Behavior*, 6, 575-583.

Hoghughi, M. (1992). *Assessing child and adolescent disorders: A practice manual*. Newbury Park, CA: Sage.

Holden, G. W., & Miller, P. C. (1997, April). Cognitive versus emotional parenting: Alignments between child-rearing cognitions, emotions, and reported behavior. Paper presented at the Biennial Meeting of the Society for Research in Child Development, Washington, DC.

Huber, M. (1981). The church as a resource. *Family Life Developments*. Ithaca: Region II Child Abuse and Neglect Resources Center.

Huesmann, L. R., Eron, L. D., & Yarmel, P. W. (1987). Intellectual functioning and aggression. *Journal of Personality and Social Psychology*, 52, 232-240.

Huchings, N. (1988). *The violent family*. New York: Human Sciences Press.

Hyman, I. (1997). *The Case Against Spanking: How to Discipline Your Child Without Hitting*. San Francisco: Jossey Bass Publishers.

Isen, A. M., & Levin, P. F. (1972). The effect of feeling good on helping: Cookies and kindness. *Journal of Personality and Social Psychology*, 21, 384-388.

Johnson, T. (1996). *The Sexual Dangers of Spanking Children*. Parents and Teachers Against Violence in Education. P. O. Box 1033, Alamo, CA 94507.

Joubert, C. E. (1990). Relationship among self-esteem, psychological reactance, and other personality variables. *Psychological Reports*, 66, 1147-1151.

Joubert, C. E. (1992). Antecedents of narcissism and psychological reactance as indicated by college students' retrospective reports of their parents' behaviors. *Psychological Reports*, 70, 1111-1115.

Journal of Sex Research. (1987). Society for the Scientific Study of Sexuality. Allentown, PA.

Kadushin, A. & Martin, J. (1981). *Child abuse: an interactional event*. New York: Columbia University Press.

Kahn, M. (1966). The physiology of catharsis. *Journal of Personality and Social Psychology*, 3, 278-298.

Kandel, D. B. (1990). Parenting styles, drug use, and children's adjustment in families of young adults. *Journal of*

Marriage and the Family, 52, 183-196.

Kazdin, Z. E. (1987). Treatment of antisocial behavior in children: Current status and future directions. *Psychological Bulletin*, 102, 187-203.

Kingsley, V. C. (1969). The effects of the double bind conflict and sex of the experimenter on the conceptual functioning and visual discrimination of male good and poor premorbid schizophrenics. Doctoral Dissertation, New York University, University Microfilms 70-16, 078.

Kinsey, A. C., Pomeroy, W. B., & Martin, C. E. (1948). *Sexual behavior in the human male*. Philadelphia: W. B. Saunders.

Kirby, J. S., Chu, J. A., & Dill, D. L. (1993). Correlates of dissociative symptomatology in patients with physical and sexual abuse histories. *Comprehensive Psychiatry*, 34, 258-263.

Kohlberg, L. (1964). Development of Moral Character and Moral Idealogy. In M.L. Hoffman & L.W. Hoffman (Eds). Review of Child Development Research (Vol. 1). New York: Russell Sage Foundation.

Kurtz, P. D., Gardin, J. M., Wodarski, J. S., & Howing, P. T. (1993). Maltreatment and the school-aged child: School performance consequences. *Journal of Child Abuse and Neglect*, 17, 581-589.

Larzelere, R. (1998). A review of the outcomes of parental use of non-abusive or customary physical punishment. *Pediatrics*, 98, 824-829.

Lepper, M. R., Green, D, & Nisbett, R. E. (1973). Undermining children's intrinsic interest with extrinsic rewards. *Journal of Personality and Social Psychology*, 28, 129-137.

Linden, D. R. (1976). The effect of intensity and frequency of intermittent punishment in acquisition on resistance to extinction of an approach response in the rat. *Animal Learning and Behavior*, 4, 451-456.

Lovaas, I.O. & Bucher, B. (1974). *Perspectives in behavior modification with deviant children.* Englewood, NJ: Prentice-Hall, Inc.

Lovaas, & Simmons, (1969). Self-Mutilation by Autistic Children and Two Procedures for Eliminating It. *Journal of Applied Behavior Analysis, 2,* 143-157.

Maccoby, E. E., & Martin, J. A. (1983). Socialization in the context of the family: Parent-child interaction in E. Mravis Hetherington (ed.), *Handbook of Child Psychology* (Vol. 4). *Socialization, Personality and Social Development.* New York: Wiley.

MacKeith, R. (1974). Speculations on non-accidental injury as a cause of chronic brain disorder. *Developmental Medicine and Child Neurology,* 16, 216-218.

Marion, M. (1982). Primary prevention of child abuse" The role of the family life educator. *Family Relations,* 31, 575-581.

Mattiace, P. (February 3, 1995). Poll: Spanking okay, but don't hit wife. The Associated Press.

Maurer, A. & Wallerstein, J. S. (1985). *The Bible and the Rod.* The Committee to End Violence in the Next Generation. 977 Keeler Ave. Berkeley, CA 94708.

McBurney, D. H. (1996). *How to think like a psychologist: Critical thinking in psychology.* Upper Saddle River, NJ: Prentice Hall.

McCord, J. (1996). Unintended consequences of punishment. *Pediatrics,* 98, 832-835.

McMillan, H. et al. (1999). Slapping and spanking in childhood and its association with lifetime prevalence of psychiatric disorders in a general population sample. *Canadian Medical Association Journal.*

Miller, R. L., Brickman, P., & Bolen, D. (1975). Attribution versus persuasion as a means for modifying behavior. *Journal of Personality and Social Psychology,* 31, 430-441.

Miller, D. L., & Kelly, M. L. (1992). Treatment acceptability: The effects of parent gender, marital adjustment, and child behavior. *Child & Family Behavior Therapy*, 14, 11-23.

Miller, D. T., & Ross, M. (1975). Self-serving biases in the attribution of causality: Fact or fiction? *Psychological Bulletin*, 82, 213-225.

Money, J. (1987). Masochism: On the childhood origin of paraphilia, opponent-process theory, and antiandrogen therapy. *The Journal of Sex Research*, 23, 273-275.

Moore, D. W. & Straus, M. A. (1987). *Violence of Parents Toward Their Children*. Report submitted to the New Hampshire Task Force on Child Abuse and Neglect. Durham, NH: Family Research Laboratory, University of New Hampshire.

Myers, D. (1992). *The Pursuit of Happiness: Who is Happy and Why*. New York: Morrow.

Myers, D. (2002). *Social Psychology*, New York: McGraw-Hill.

National PTA. (1991). Corporal punishment—myths and realities. National PTA. Chicago.

Norris, J. (1989). *Serial Killers*. New York: Anchor.

Oates, R. K., Forrest, D., & Peacock, A. (1985). Self esteem of abused children. *Journal of Child Abuse and Neglect*, 9, 159-163.

Olweus, D. (1978). *Aggression in the schools: Bullies and whipping boys*. Washington, DC: Hemisphere.

Olweus, D. (1979). Stability of aggressive reaction patterns in males: A review. *Psychological Bulletin*, 86, 852-875.

Olweus, D. (1980). Familial and temperamental determinants of aggressive behavior in adolescent boys: A causal analysis. *Developmental Psychology*, 19, 257-268.

Olweus, D. (1991). Bully/victim problems among school children: Basic facts and effects of a school-based intervention program. In D. Pepler & K. Rubin (Eds.), *The development and treatment of childhood aggression* (pp 41-448).

Hillsdale, NJ: Erlbaum.

Owens, D. J., & Straus, M. A. (1975). *Aggressive Behavior, Volume 1*. Alan R. Liss, Inc.

Paintal, S. (1999). Banning corporal punishment of children. *Childhood Education*, 3, 36-39.

Painter, S. L., & Dutton, D. (1981). Traumatic bonding: The development of emotional attachments in battered women and other relationships of intermittent abuse. *Victimology*, 6, 139-155.

Patterson, G. R. (1982a). The management and disruption of families. *Coercive Family Process*. Eugene, OR: Castalia.

Patterson, G. R. (1982b). A Social Learning Approach to Family Intervention: III. *Coercive Family Process*. Eugene, OR: Castalia.

Patterson, B. R., DeBaryshe, B. D., & Ramsey, E. (1989). A developmental perspective on antisocial behavior. *American Psychologist*, 44, 329-335.

Pelzer, D. (1995). *A Child Called It: One Child's Courage to Survive*. Health Communications.

Piaget, J. (1952). The Origins of Intelligence in Children. New York: International University Press.

Piaget, J. (1967). *Six psychological studies*. New York: Random House.

Power, T. G., & Chapieski, M. L. (1986). Childrearing and impulse control in toddlers: A naturalistic investigation. *Developmental Psychology*, 22, 271-275.

ReligiousTolerance.org (1999). Child corporal punishment: Spanking. *World Wide Web* site p. 4. INTERNET

Reuters. (August 3, 1998). Want smarter kids? Don't spank them. Washington.

Riak, J. (2002). Personal communication.

Rice, D.P. & Miller, L.S. (1993). The economic burden of affective disorders. *Advances in Health Economics and Health Services Research*. Edited by R.M. Scheffler and L.F. Rossiter, Vol. 14. JAI Press Inc. pp. 37-54.

Roberts, M. (1990). Adjusting chair timeout enforcement procedures for oppositional children. *Behavior Therapy, 21,* 257-271.

Rogers, C. (1954). Towards a theory of creativity. *ETC: A Review of General Semantics,* 11, 249-260.

Rohner, R. P., & Bourque, S. L. (1996). Children's perceptions of corporal punishment, caretaker acceptance, and psychological adjustment in a poor, biracial Southern community. *Journal of Marriage and the Family,* 58, 842-853.

Sacramento Bee. (March 26, 1995). Girl forced to disrobe, then paddled at school, police say. Sacramento.

Salzinger, S., Feldman, R. S., Hammer, M., & Rosario, M. (1993). The effects of physical abuse on children's social relationships. *Journal of Child Development,* 64, 169-187.

Samenow, S. (1984). *Inside the criminal mind.* NY: Times Books/Random House.

Sears, R. R., Maccoby, E. C., & Levin, H. (1957). *Patterns of Child Rearing.* Evanston: Row Peterson.

Schwartz, B. (1989). *Psychology of learning and behavior.* (2nd ed.) New York: Norton.

Sedlak, A.J. & Broadhurst, D.D. (1996). *Third national incidence study of child abuse and neglect.* U.S. DHHS National Center on Child Abuse and Neglect.

Shulins, N. (June 29, 1986). Children turned killers: How do lives go so wrong so soon. The Associated Press.

Simon, W. (1972). Some sociometric evidence for validity of Coopersmith's Self-esteem Inventory. *Perceptual and Motor Skills,* 34, 93-94.

Simons, R. J., Johnson, C., & Conger, R. D. (1994). Harsh corporal punishment, perceived caretaker warmth, and cultural beliefs on the psychological adjustment of children in St. Kitts, West Indies. *Journal of Marriage and the Family,* 53, 681-694.

Sinykin, S.C. (March 1983). The no-nagging, no-yelling, no-spanking method of discipline that worked for us. *REDBOOK Magazine*, 26-27.

Skinner, B.F. (1972). Humanism and behaviorism. *The Humanist*, 32, 18-20.

Skinner, B.F. (1976). *Walden Two*. Englewood Cliffs, NJ: Prentice Hall.

Sollenberger, R. T. (1968). Chinese-American child-rearing practices and juvenile delinquency. *Journal of Social Psychology*, 74, 13-23.

Steele, B. F., & Pollack, C. B. (1968). A psychiatric study of parents who abuse infants and small children. In Helfer, R. E. and Kempe, C. H. (Eds.). *The Battered Child*. Chicago: The University of Chicago Press.

Straus, M. A. (1983). Corporal punishment, child abuse, and wife beating: What do they all have in common? in the *Dark Side of Families: Current Family Violence Research*, edited by Finkelhor, D., Gelles, R. J., Hotaling, B. T., & Straus, M. A. Newbury Park, CA: Sage Publishers.

Straus, M. A. (1991). Discipline and deviance: Physical punishment of children and violence and other crime in adulthood. *Social Problems*, 38, 131-149.

Straus, M. A. (1994). *Beating the devil out of them: Corporal punishment in American Families*. New York: Lexington Books.

Straus, M. A. (1996). Spanking and the making of a violent society. *Pediatrics*, 98, 837-842.

Straus, M.A. (2000). *Beating the Devil out of Them: Corporal Punishment in American Families and Its Effects on Children, 2nd Edition*. New Brunswick, NJ: Transaction Publishers.

Straus, M. A. (2000). Corporal punishment by parents: The cradle of violence in the family and society. *The Virginia*

Journal of Social Policy and the Law.

Straus, M. A., & Donnelly, D. A. (1993). Corporal punishment of adolescents by American parents. *Youth and Society*, 24, 419-443.

Straus, M. A., & Gelles, R. J. (1986). Societal change and change in family violence from 1975 to 1985 as revealed by two national surveys. *Journal of Marriage and the Family*, 48, 465-480.

Straus, M. A., & Gelles, R. J., & Steinmetz, S. K. (1980). *Behind closed doors: Violence in the American Family*. New York: Doubleday/Anchor.

Straus, M. A., & Gimpel, H. S. (1992, August). Corporal punishment by parents and economic achievement: A theoretical model and some preliminary empirical data. Paper presented at the annual meeting of the American Sociological Association, Pittsburgh, PA.

Straus, M. A., & Hill, K. A. (1997, July 1). *Corporal punishment, child-to-parent bonding, and delinquency*. Paper presented at the 5th International Family Violence Research Conference, Durham, NH: Family Research Laboratory, University of New Hampshire.

Straus, M. A., & Kantor, G. K. (1994). Corporal punishment of adolescents by parents: A risk factor in the epidemiology of depression, suicide, alcohol abuse, child abuse, and wife beating. *Adolescence*, 29, 545-561.

Straus, M. A., & Kantor, G. K. (1995). Trends in physical abuse by parents from 1975 to 1992: A comparison of three national surveys. Paper presented at the annual meeting of the American Society of Criminology, Boston, Nov. 18.

Straus, M. A., & Mathur, A. K. (April, 1995). Corporal punishment and children's academic achievement. Paper presented at the annual meeting of the Pacific Sociological Society, San Francisco.

Straus, M. A., & Mouradian, V. E. (1998). Impulsive corporal punishment by mothers and antisocial behavior and impulsiveness of children, *Behavioral Sciences and the Law,* 16, 353-374.

Straus, M. A., & Moynihan (1994). Who spanks the most? In Straus, M. A. (1994). *Beating the devil out of them: Corporal punishment in American Families.* 49-63. New York: Lexington Books.

Straus, M. A., & Paschall, M. J. (1998). Corporal punishment by mothers and child's cognitive development: A longitudinal study. Paper presented at the 14th World Conference of Sociology, Montreal, Canada.

Straus, M. A., Sugarman, D. B., & Giles-Sims (1997). Corporal punishment by parents and subsequent antisocial behavior of children. *Archives of Pediatrics and Adolescent Medicine,* 155, 761-767.

Straus, M. A., & Yodanis, C. L. (1995). Corporal punishment by parents: Implications for primary prevention of assaults on spouses and children. *The University of Chicago Law School Roundtable,* 2, 35-66.

Sapp, A. D., & Carter, D. L. (1978). *Child abuse in Texas: A descriptive study of Texas residents' attitudes.* Huntsville: Sam Houston State University.

Thompson, E. E. (1999). The short- and long-term effects of corporal punishment on children: A meta-analytic review. *Psychological Bulletin, .*

Trumbull, D. A., & Ravenel, S. D. (1996). Spare the rod? New research challenges spanking critics. *Family Policy,* 9

Turner, H. A., & Finkelhor, D. (1996). Corporal punishment as a stressor among youth. *Journal of Marriage and the Family,* 58, 155-166.

Ulrich, R. E. & Azrin, N. H. (1966). Reflexive fighting in response to aversive stimulation. In Verhave, T. (Ed.) *The Experimental Analysis of Behavior.* New York: Appleton-Century-Crofts.

UPI. (1986). Family life dangerous. New York.

U.S. Supreme Court. (1977). Ingraham vs. Wright 490 U.S. 651.

USA Today. (December 7, 1995). Child abuse estimates low. McLean, VA: Gannett Co, Inc.

Watson, G. (1957). Some personality differences in children related to strict or permissive parental discipline. *Journal of Psychology, 44,* 227-249.

Wauchope, B. & Straus, M. (1990). Physical punishment and physical abuse of American children: Incidence rates by age, gender, and occupational class. In *Physical Violence in American Families.* Straus, M. & Gelles, R. (Eds.) New Brunswick, NJ: Transaction Publishers.

Welsh, R. S. (1976). Severe parental punishment and delinquency: A developmental theory. *Journal of Clinical Child Psychology, 5,* 17-21.

Welsh, R. S. (1978). Severe parental punishment and aggression: The link between corporal punishment and delinquency. In Hyman, I. A. and Wise, James H. (1979). *Corporal Punishment in American Education: Readings in History, Practice and Alternatives.* Philadelphia: Temple University Press.

Westat Inc. (1993). A report on the maltreatment of children with disabilities. Washington, DC: National Center for Child Abuse and Neglect.

Wheeling Intelligencer. (May 27, 1994). Caning is proposed. Wheeling, WV: Ogden Publishers.

Whiting, B. (ed.). (1963). *Six cultures.* New York: Wiley.

Whitmore, E. A., Kramer, J. R., & Knutson, J. F. (1993). The association between punitive childhood experience and hyperactivity. *Child Abuse and Neglect,* 17, 357-366.

Widom, C. S. (1989a). The cycle of violence. *Science,* 244, 160-166.

Widom, C. S. (1989b). Does violence beget violence? A critical examination of the literature. *Psychological Bulletin,* 106, 3-28.

Wilson, J. Q., & Herrnstein, R. J. (1986) *Crime and Human Nature*. New York: Simon and Schuster.

Windell, J. (1993). 20 discipline strategies that really work. *Parent's Digest, Summer*, 90-92.

Wolak, J. (1996). Patterns of parental control and sibling violence. *Sibling Violence Review*, 1, 1-18.

Ziegert, K. A. (1983). The Wedesih prohibition of corporal punishment: A preliminary report. *Journal of Marriage and the Family*, 45, 917-926.

Zigler, E., & Hall, N. W. (1989). Physical child abuse in America: Past, present, and future. In D. Cicchetti & V. Carlson (Eds.), *Child Maltreatment: Theory and Research on the Causes and Consequences of Child Abuse and Neglect* (pp. 38-73). Cambridge: Cambridge University Press.

Zimbardo, P. (1977). *Shyness*. Reading, MA: Addison-Wesley.

Index

additive, 122-123
delay effects
harsh, 75-76
honesty
impulsive, 153
inconsistent, 132
mild, 73, 76
motives, 122
severe, 10, 80
sub-abusive, 39
subtractive, 122-124

R

Rats
stereotypical fighting posture, 32
Redirection, 143
Regression toward the mean, 105-106
Reinforcement:
extrinsic, 140-141
intermittent, 127
intrinsic, 140-141
negative, 107, 129-131
positive, 120-122, 142, 153
Response cost, 124
Revocation of privileges
Riots, prison:
Attica, 34
Lucasville, 34
New Mexico, 34
Romeo and Juliet effect, 69

S

Search for Extra-Terrestrial Intelligence (SETI), 162
Self justification, 73, 90-91, 140
Self serving bias
Serial killers, 40
Shakespeare, 181
Skinner box, 31
Social trap, 107-108
Sociopath
Spanking:
achievement
alienation, 47-50
antisocial behavior, 52-55
anxiety, 47
as a cultural norm, 9-15, 179-180
biblical interpretation , 180-182
bonding and attachment, 48
creativity, 51
crime, 40
depression, 45, 46, 47
guilt, 103
harmful side effects list, 24-26
intelligence, 63
juvenile delinquency, 41
learning, 62-64
negative affect, 24

About the Author

Michael J. Marshall is a Professor of Psychology at West Liberty State College and a licensed clinical psychologist in private practice. Dr. Marshall lives with his wife, son, and three daughters in Wheeling, West Virginia. He was born in Los Angeles in 1949, the son of an LAPD police officer. After a two year stint in the Navy during the Vietnam War, during which he served on a nuclear submarine, he resumed his education at California State University. He worked his way through school as a swimming pool contractor in Southern California. After receiving his BA and MA in psychology, he entered a doctoral program at Claremont Graduate University where he completed his PhD in psychology in 1987. He taught at High Point University and North Carolina A&T State University until 1992 when he became a faculty member at West Liberty State College, where he currently teaches applied psychology.

He is the author of a dozen scholarly research articles in psychology, published in journals ranging from the *International Journal of Addictions* to *The Journal of*

Psychological Practice. He has considerable clinical experience working with parolees, substance abusers, and patients with psychotic and emotional disorders. He has a private practice and does community mental health contract work. His duties include assessment, treatment planning, crisis stabilization, and psychotherapy. He often testifies as an expert witness in civil commitment proceedings. In addition to lecturing and seeing patients, he conducts Continuing Education workshops for mental health professionals and does research on addictions and family discipline practices. He has been honored for his professional work with awards in the areas of professional achievement, outstanding service, and excellence in research.

Marshall drew on his professional knowledge, research, and experience to help him write *Why Spanking Doesn't Work.* He believes hitting is more of an emotional impediment to overcome rather than a means of proper socialization. His suspicions were professionally confirmed upon becoming familiar with the corporal punishment research literature as a psychologist. He drew his inspiration for popularizing alternative discipline strategies from such disparate sources as the pioneering family research of Sociologist Murray A. Straus, PhD, author of *Beating the Devil Out of Them* and the superior gentle horse training techniques of Monty Roberts, author of *The Man Who Listens to Horses.* Marshall took Straus's words that "The best kept secret in developmental psychology is the harmful effects of corporal punishment" as a battle cry for the duty to inform parents of the hidden dangers inherent in their decision to use the paddle.

Marshall spends his leisure time working on his old three story house, listening to classical music, playing racquetball, and traveling and camping across the country with his family during summer vacations.